SEVEN PRACTICES OF HEALTHY YOUTH MINISTRY

THE
LUTHERAN CHURCH
MISSOURI SYNOD
Youth Ministry

CONCORDIA PUBLISHING HOUSE • SAINT LOUIS

Published by Concordia Publishing House
3558 S. Jefferson Ave., St. Louis, MO 63118-3968
1-800-325-3040 • cph.org

Manufactured in China/055760/101244

1 2 3 4 5 6 7 8 9 10   32 31 30 29 28 27 26 25 24 23

CONTENTS

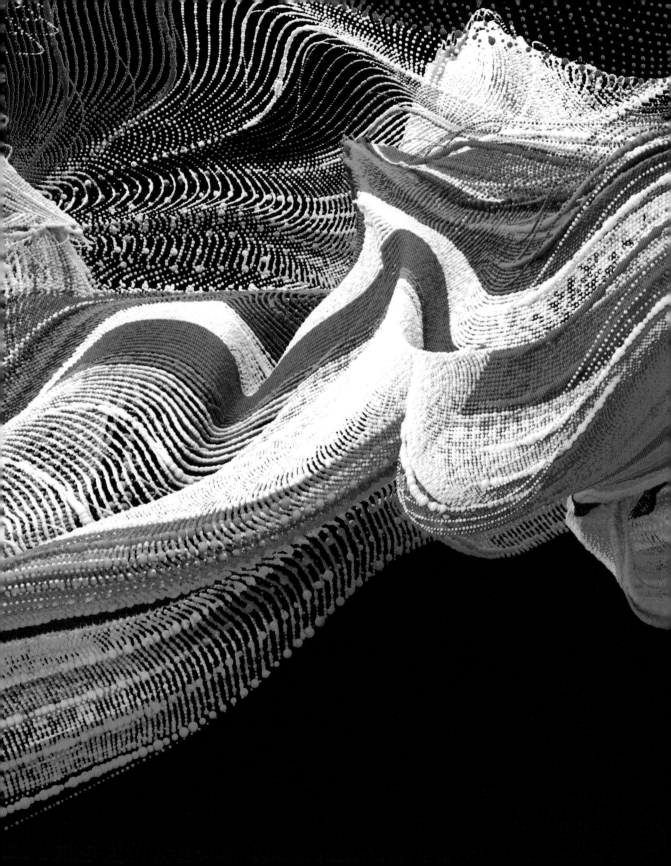

Introduction

Seven Practices of Healthy Youth Ministry was designed by the office of The Lutheran Church—Missouri Synod Youth Ministry for use in LCMS youth ministries. While the LCMS Office of National Mission—Youth Ministry staff played a role in its development, this book was written by Rev. Dr. Mark Kiessling and Julianna Shults.

Julianna, a director of Christian education, serves as program manager for resources and leadership with LCMS Youth Ministry. Her work includes managing youthesource.com and LCMS YouthLead along with other research and resourcing. She supports adult leaders at the LCMS Youth Gathering and often speaks at district and other church conferences about service, leadership, and generational data. Julianna is a graduate of Concordia University, Nebraska and Loyola University Chicago. She has also completed training from the Karpenko Institute for Nurturing and Developing Leadership Excellence.

Mark serves as director of LCMS Youth Ministry. In that role, he supports the leadership, service, resourcing, and networking functions of LCMS Youth Ministry. Before serving as director, He was associate director in charge of the LCMS Youth Gathering. Mark graduated from Concordia Seminary, St. Louis in 2006. He was awarded an honorary doctor of letters from Concordia Seminary, St. Louis and an honorary doctor of law from Concordia University Chicago.

As a part of the LCMS Youth Ministry staff, Mark and Julianna cohost the podcast *End Goals* on KFUO radio.

Acknowledgments

We want to thank the research team for the 2017–2018 "Millennials and the LCMS" study. This includes Ryan Curnutt, senior research analyst at LCMS Research Services; Kevin Borchers, DCE, PhD; and Dave Rueter, DCE, PhD.

This book would not have been possible without numerous staff members of The Lutheran Church—Missouri Synod. Thank you to the present and previous staff of LCMS Youth Ministry, who listened to presentations over and over, made suggestions, provided encouragement, and created great resources. Thank you, Meredith Whitefield Smith, Krista Miller, Jim Lohman, Renee Lorenz, Derek Broten, and Terry Dittmer for your contributions and critiques.

Thank you to the numerous leaders on Concordia University and Seminary campuses and LCMS districts who invited us to present or reviewed copy as we prepared the seven practices. We can't count the number of LCMS youth workers who provided insight and encouragement as we sought input and narrowed the practices. We especially want to thank those who were trained and presented on the challenges in 2021 and 2022. Thank you for challenging us and helping us think through a number of matters. Thank you, Rev. Ben Meyer; DCEs Maddie Gong, Cheri Selander, Christine Ekberg, and Peter Hiller; DCM Blake Brockman; and Deac. Heidi Goehmann.

Thank you to the team at Concordia Publishing House for making this book possible through your gifts of editing, graphic design and layout, project management, printing, and distributing.

Julianna: I would also like to thank my parents, Rick and Marilyn Shults, for modeling Christ-centered servant leadership not just for our family but for so many young people in the church. Thanks to my sister, Christina, and her husband, James, for your examples of hospitality, service, warmth, challenge, and grace. Thank you to the staff and members of Faith Lutheran in Topeka, Kansas; Hope Lutheran in Plant City, Florida; St. Paul Lutheran in Chicago; and Christ Memorial in St. Louis, who shaped me and this book. Thank you to DCE Jim Bradshaw, Rev. Dr. Mark Kiessling, and countless other mentors for taking a risk and investing in me. I'm hoping you think it paid off.

Mark: I would like to thank my wife, Beth, for her love, support, and patience. Also, thank you, Mom and Dad, Richard and Maxine Kiessling, for being engaged parents who constantly showed me Jesus' grace. Thanks to my sisters, Julie Liedtke and Jill Davitt, for showing me love and forgiveness I don't deserve. Thank you to the saints at Grace Lutheran Church in Hamilton, Montana, who were amazing supportive adults and peers to this young disciple of Jesus. Specifically, thank you to Bob Baker, my youth director, who showed me Christ's love and compassion while encouraging me in my life with Christ. (I needed it!)

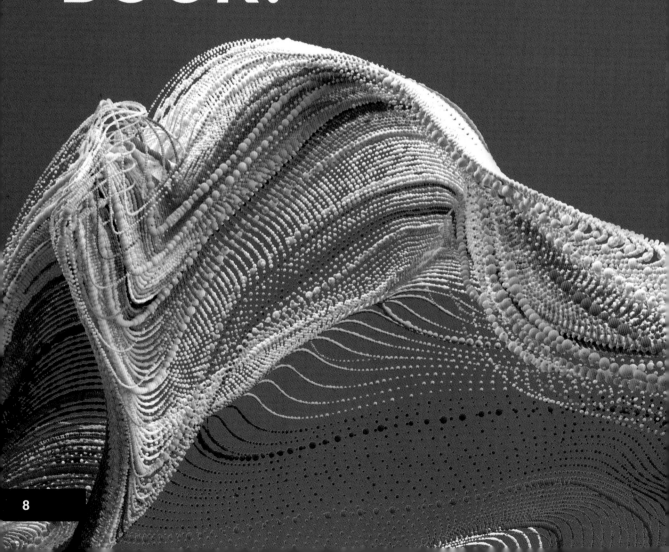

Chapter 1

WHY ANOTHER YOUTH MINISTRY BOOK?

It started with questions—lots of questions. In our office at LCMS Youth Ministry, we receive regular emails, phone calls, and occasionally even faxes from youth leaders who ask questions around a common theme:

"I'm in charge of youth ministry. Now, where do I start?"

"How do I know if our youth ministry is healthy and doing the right things to care for our teens?"

"My youth ministry is dwindling. What should I be doing differently?"

"What is youth ministry supposed to look like?"

Over the years, we have heard from a wide variety of youth leaders. Some were newly elected to the youth board and trying to figure out a first step. Others had been doing youth ministry for twice as long as the teens they serve have been alive. Some were naturally drawn to teens; others took a bit of warming up. Some questions came from trained professional church workers who focused on youth ministry; others were volunteers.

Parents, young adults, retirees, pastors, DCEs, and more are all deeply committed to filling this vital role in their congregation. They reached out to us for insight and resources to help them in the task of caring for young people. In doing so, we saw their love for the teens in their congregations and communities. Behind every email, Facebook message, and phone call was a servant heart that wanted young people to know Jesus.

Questions come to us a bit removed from their contexts. We often don't know the youth leader or the young people. Youth leaders reach out with requests arising from a deep commitment to their vocations. They know each young person by name. Perhaps they were even there to witness some of these teens receive God's gift of faith and forgiveness given in Baptism. They have been in a congregational community praying and supporting as children grow into teens. Parents and youth leaders know the value of youth ministry as teens face new challenges to their faith. Youth leaders take how the Spirit empowers them to teach, listen, engage, and mentor youth in this critical time seriously.

In each question to our office, we caught a glimpse of the church's desire for teens to be disciples of Jesus now and into eternity. We know youth leaders are praying regularly for God's wisdom and the Holy Spirit to guide them. They stay up late thinking about how they can best support the faith lives of teens. They read articles and talk to other pastors and youth leaders. Through constant assessment, they strive to meet youth in the congregation and community where they are at with the love of Jesus. Youth ministry constantly changes as teens join and grow and the culture shifts. Even in the best of circumstances, healthy youth ministry can seem like a nebulous task.

> I have no greater joy than to hear that my children are walking in the truth. (3 John 4)

One thing all youth leaders share is that they take no greater joy than to see young people who are walking in the truth of Jesus.

HEALTHY YOUTH MINISTRY REALLY DOES BOIL DOWN TO SHARING THE GOSPEL WITH TEENS, AND THAT IS AN ANSWER THAT WILL NEVER CHANGE. IT'S NOT SURPRISING OR NEW. IT IS AS IT HAS ALWAYS BEEN. WE SHARE THE SAME HEART AND PASSION AS YOUTH LEADERS—TO SEE MORE YOUNG PEOPLE IN THE SAVING FAITH OF JESUS.

So when we respond to these questions, we start with what is most important. In many ways, our response is the same as it's always been: saving faith in Jesus through His death and resurrection. Healthy youth ministry really does boil down to sharing the Gospel with teens, and that is an answer that will never change. It's not surprising or new. It is as it has always been. We share the same heart and passion as youth leaders—to see more young people in the saving faith of Jesus.

Beyond that, we are learners who are constantly seeking better ways to respond to the questions around healthy youth ministry. In our roles, we get the joy of supporting, resourcing, and cheering on youth leaders. It is a gift to observe healthy youth ministry in LCMS congregations of different sizes and contexts. We celebrate when congregations and individual youth leaders impact the lives of young people, including when the Holy Spirit leads our youth to careers in church work. Every year, we get to see young people who have been supported by youth leaders discover more about themselves and their vocations. There is much to celebrate.

When we see healthy youth ministry, we gather stories and data so that we can share what we learn with others. As we see healthy youth ministry flourish, we take keen notes so we can relay best practices that can be used in other places. We constantly study new research and ideas. We listen well to youth, parents, and church leaders for key takeaways. We also seek out experts in youth ministry to ask our own questions of those wiser and more experienced than we are. It's a task we don't take lightly. We hope these observations, resources, and data give us insight we can share to help the church.

Over and again, youth leaders reach out with questions that focus on programs, relationships, development, structure, and environment, all informed by the Gospel. These kinds of questions have been asked of those serving in our Youth Ministry office for many years. Over those years, the responses and resources we've suggested have changed. In some eras, we might have encouraged youth leaders to join a larger youth ministry organization. In others, past staff might have provided them with a more systematic and programmatic handbook of ways to support young people. Or we may have shared books and articles by other youth ministry leaders.

We reached a point where we no longer felt like we had a clear, concise, and practical response. We noticed a growing discontent with how we replied to these questions. With God's help, we did our best, but we knew we needed to formulate something that was faithful, research-driven, and practical. We wanted a better response to the question of healthy youth ministry for ourselves so that we could share it with others.

We heard you, and we share your deep desire to see the young people you love walking in faith. So we began to develop our response.

Where to Find a New Response

Answers to big questions like this are not easy to develop. It took us years as we sought out many different important sources. Together, the staff at LCMS Youth Ministry listened to youth and youth ministry leaders, examined data, and dug into Scripture and Lutheran doctrine. We investigated with our own research. We had long discussions and debates over wording, order, and priorities. We wanted a way to articulate what was key for healthy congregational youth ministry—around which we could build our own programming and share with excitement. From this work, *Seven Practices of Healthy Youth Ministry* was formed.

We first turned to Scripture. God's Word to us is the center of all congregational ministry, including youth ministry. In looking at Scripture, we can see who God is and what God has done for us and our young people. We base our faith, hope, and ministry on God's living and active Word above all else. There is nowhere else we can go but to the Bible to define what God has called us to do in caring for young people.

Throughout the Old and New Testaments, God gives direction on how we are to care for and teach young people. In Deuteronomy 6, God commanded the people of Israel to teach their children as they went along throughout their day. We see young people like Samuel and David stepping out in faith to do great things empowered by God's Holy Spirit. In Luke 18, Jesus told the disciples to let the children come to Him and not to hinder them. We see people both young and old sharing the Good News of salvation through Jesus in the Epistles.

> IT IS NOT SURPRISING THAT IN OUR LUTHERAN THEOLOGY, AS IN SCRIPTURE, WE HEAR OF THE IMPORTANCE OF YOUNG PEOPLE IN THE CHURCH AND HOW WE ENCOURAGE THEM IN THEIR LIVES OF FAITH.

We found powerful instruction in our Lutheran theology as well. What we believe as Lutherans comes from God's Word, and it gives important language and understanding to what we teach young people. Our understanding of Baptism, vocation, the role of parents, and the distinction between Law and Gospel all informed how we defined healthy youth ministry. It is not surprising that in our Lutheran theology, as in Scripture, we hear of the importance of young people in the church and how we encourage them in their lives of faith.

We looked at research from reliable sources that have studied Christians and the church for many years. There are many components of the seven practices that you might hear from other sources. One of the things we wanted to do with the seven practices was to create a single place where we could synthesize different insights on healthy youth ministry that have been highlighted by others. Yet we wanted to give these a uniquely Lutheran perspective.

We do our very best to give credit to the original sources for research and ideas. Two that you will see most often are Fuller Youth Institute and The Barna Group research. Fuller's data and application in *Sticky Faith* and *Growing Young* played a tremendous role in helping shape some of the seven practices. In fact, we took certain components, like the suggested number of supportive adults for each individual youth, directly from their work. Barna also gave us key research that helped us translate what we know about millennials to Generation Z. In the past few years, Barna has worked in partnership with Lutheran Hour Ministries on several important research projects, including what makes a spiritually vibrant household.

However, the most important research projects we pulled from were our own. The Lutheran Church—Missouri Synod has a wealth of information from the annual LCMS reporting statistics. LCMS Youth Ministry has conducted research since the very first LCMS Youth Gathering in 1980. Rev. Dr. Terry Dittmer, the previous director of LCMS Youth Ministry, started polling young people who attended Youth Gatherings to get a sampling of the attitudes, beliefs, and interests of teens in the church. We have continued that poll for more than forty years with every LCMS Youth Gathering. While the poll is not taken by a large or random enough sample to make wide statements about LCMS teens, it does give us a glimpse into their thoughts and values.

In 2016, LCMS Youth Ministry began a research endeavor that was bigger than any before: a three-part research project on millennials and the LCMS. In the first phase, congregations were randomly invited to complete a survey. The survey contained questions about the congregation's program and context, then focused specifically on the confirmation classes of 2004–6. Assuming the standard confirmation age of twelve to fourteen years old, these young people would have been twenty-three to twenty-seven years old at the time of the study. Since many of the existing pastors or DCEs were not at their congregations during those years, respondents were encouraged to recruit help from staff or parents who might know more about these millennials.

Our second phase was an online survey of millennials who were in their twenties and who had grown up in the LCMS. The survey took about twenty minutes to complete and included questions about the millennials' lives, families, current faith practices, and theology. More than two thousand young adults took the survey, both those who had stayed active in the LCMS and those who grew up in the LCMS but had since left it. This was far more data than we ever expected, and we took listening to these young people very seriously.

In the fall of 2017, we followed up our survey with our third phase, which consisted of several focus groups that allowed us to get even more insight into some of the data we found in the survey. We chose questions that would help us better understand some of the data we saw around the need for peer support in young adulthood, what welcome and warmth meant, and more. These conversations helped us to better understand the statistical data we received in the survey. We captured what we found in this research in the book *Relationships Count: Engaging and*

Retaining Millennials, and you will see many references to that research throughout this book.

Last, but certainly not least, we talked to experienced youth leaders. LCMS Youth Ministry is blessed to have a network of youth leaders, both professional and lay, who are willing to share from their depth of wisdom and experience. While data and research are helpful, the seven practices needed to be practical. For us to develop something that wouldn't just work in theory, we spoke with those who are on the ground working with teens and their families every day. We also asked for input from those who train people at our Concordia Universities. We tried to listen well to their wisdom, and you will hear their stories throughout this book. If you have been around youth ministry for a while, we hope much of what you read here resonates with what you are already doing in youth ministry.

The seven practices have changed since we first laid them out. We adjusted language and focus as we started to see youth ministry in our own congregations through the lens of the seven practices. As we presented them to more youth leaders, we listened to feedback and clarified concepts. It was a beautiful thing to hear leaders share where they saw the seven practices in the Bible and as they served young people. Their perspectives and insights continue to guide us even now. While the seven practices may yet still change, we hope we have come to a place of confidence that we have a clear, biblical, and practical way of answering key questions about what healthy congregational youth ministry looks like.

THE SEVEN PRACTICES OF HEALTHY YOUTH MINISTRY

CONGREGATIONS HAVE . . .

Warmth, challenge, and grace

Supportive adults

Engaged parents

Opportunities to serve and lead

CONGREGATIONS HELP ALL YOUNG PEOPLE . . .

Deeply understand their baptismal faith

Develop a resilient identity in Christ

Live out their unique vocation

What the Seven Practices Are Not

While the practices described here may not cover every facet of ministry or teaching in the church, we do hope they provide support, direction, and inspiration. Before you dive into this material, we want to highlight four things you will not see in our seven practices of healthy youth ministry:

1. This is not a program.

Believe us, this would be a whole lot easier if there was one single program that, when implemented, guaranteed 100 percent of the young people of your congregation would grow as disciples of Jesus for life. During our research project with millennials and the LCMS, we even included a variety of questions in an attempt to find programmatic solutions to the problem of retention. Alas, there is no single program, staffing, or resource that will ensure healthy youth ministry.

The seven practices will not present you with a curriculum, schedule, or plan of events. Instead, the focus is on relationships: God's relationship with us, parents' relationships with their children, the congregational relationship with youth, youths' relationship with key adults, and youths' relationships with peers. We believe that when you seek to build and sustain relationships, the right programs for your congregation will become clear. This also means that implementing the seven practices will look dramatically different in every congregation. It is up to you to find how these practices are best accomplished for your specific youth ministry.

> WE BELIEVE THAT WHEN YOU SEEK TO BUILD AND SUSTAIN RELATIONSHIPS, THE RIGHT PROGRAMS FOR YOUR CONGREGATION WILL BECOME CLEAR.

We wanted the seven practices to be descriptive, not prescriptive. If you were hoping that this book would give you five quick tricks or tips for a healthy youth ministry, you have come to the wrong place. It is not about finding the right program, curriculum, or structure that will change your youth ministry for the better. There are very few hard and fast rules. Instead, we are going to describe the trajectory your youth ministry should be following. By God's grace, you can move toward the seven practices in any way that works for you.

2. This is not a short-term fix.

One of the things you learn when making bread is that you should not rush the rise. The dough proofs after you put all the ingredients together, and that process takes time. Time allows for better flavor and structure that will provide a better outcome in the end. Sure, there are ways to speed it along, but in the end, the result is a flatter, less tasty loaf. We can think of youth ministry in the same way.

As you try to assemble the right ingredients for a healthy youth ministry, you cannot rush the process. If you do, the structural supports, relationships, resources, and culture you hope to develop will not hold together the way you hope. Instead, think of it as a slow rise process. Small actions and decisions by leaders build over time. We have our eyes open to how the Holy Spirit is at work, but we cannot force God to move on our timeline.

There will be trial and error along the way. Do not be disheartened when your work doesn't immediately result in teens flocking in droves or when you receive pushback against new ideas. At first, the changes you make might even lead to fewer people connecting with your youth ministry. Take time to ask hard questions. Be sure to keep the Gospel and your goals for youth ministry in front of you. Focus on small steps that change attitudes and environment over time. Most importantly, cover all the work in prayer. Look to God's Word for guidance for each step and stand on the solid rock of the Gospel.

Don't rush through reading this book looking just for the pieces most easily put into action. Look at it and your youth ministry holistically. It's great if you can put things into action now. You should also start conversations with leaders and parents about the long-term goals for youth ministry. Perhaps these goals will be met long after your current youth have graduated or after you no longer are leading youth ministry. Trust that God will work in and through you over time to help young people live out their faith from Baptism into adulthood.

3. This is not complicated.

As we looked at our Millennials and the LCMS research, one member of our research team said, "It is simple, but it's not easy." Over the years of research and development of the seven practices, this has continued to be true about youth ministry. The seven practices may seem overwhelming when you first encounter them, but at their core, they are simple. Do not let the number of practices or suggestions in this book lead you to make youth ministry more complicated than it needs to be.

There is a lot to unpack in the seven practices. Take your time to focus on each one. Find the places that seem like low-hanging fruit and find the natural ways you can further develop these practices in your youth ministry. Certain leaders may try to program-atize each of these practices into additional structures, volunteers, sign-ups, and trainings. Some of that can be beneficial. But before you do, be sure that the programs are serving the relationship and environment you want to develop rather than the other way around. Keep in mind that some of the best pieces of youth ministry are the simplest.

4. This isn't built by your effort.

It can be easy to believe that youth ministry succeeds or fails on the work of pastors, commissioned ministers, church staff, parents, or volunteers. That simply isn't the case. We deeply appreciate the leaders in churches who take youth ministry seriously. They pour their heart, time, and energy into caring for young people in their congregation and community. When you love the young people of your congregation, it's hard not to believe it is up to you to make sure they grow as disciples of Jesus.

The belief that it is up to us will only let us down. The truth is that it is God who is at work in and through each of us as we live out our daily vocations, including serving the youth of our congregations. It is God who works through the Word and Sacraments, giving forgiveness and new life. It is God's responsibility to give the gift of faith and sustain it. We will sin, fail, and fall short. Yet despite this, God works His will and His way in us and our youth.

There are many aspects of the seven practices that will ask you to lean into the faith that God will work through you and others. Trusting that God will show up and fulfill His promises, even when we aren't sure how that will look, is hard. Our sinful selves want to take control. Healthy youth ministry cannot be built on us—on you. It can only be built on the rock that is Jesus.

What the Seven Practices Are

You may be wondering what you will see in these practices. We hope knowing the parameters of these seven practices will help you to understand our perspective in creating them. These are a some of the encouragements we hope you see within this book:

1. This is possible for any congregation.

Julianna can remember visiting a pastor as he lamented that his congregation simply didn't have a youth ministry. The congregation only had three teenagers, so the pastor had done their confirmation in a very small group where he said they had time for great discussion alongside catechesis. As he shared about these youth, it was clear he enjoyed spending time with them. After confirmation, other adults had taken a strong interest in helping these teens find service roles that fit their unique skills. The teens didn't come every Sunday, but when they did, they joined their adult Bible study. But admittedly, there were no lock-ins, paintball outings, Superbowl parties, or any of the traditional trappings of youth programming.

As the pastor finished his description, he sighed and awaited judgment from Julianna. "It sounds to me like you have a pretty healthy and vibrant youth ministry," she responded. He was shocked because none of what his congregation did aligned with what he imagined youth ministry should be.

Size and resources matter far less to healthy youth ministry than we imagine. This congregation had given its young people opportunities to study God's Word, live out vocation, and be surrounded by adults who genuinely desired to see God at work in their lives. While there are great benefits to programming that is age-specific, there are times when many of the seven practices can be met in ways we don't expect. We have done our best to present the seven practices in a way that can be translated for any congregational setting.

No two youth ministries are going to look the same, just like no two congregations are going to look the same. Location, resources, and the level of teen involvement do not qualify or disqualify any congregation from healthy youth ministry. The devil discourages ministry by focusing our attention on limitations. Yet congregations with two or three teens or only a few resources do some of the most amazing youth ministry. Vibrant, healthy youth ministries can be found in both suburbs and in rural areas, in church plants and historic churches. Rather than comparing your youth ministry to others, your task is to find what these practices look like in your unique context. As you read, think about how you can meet your teens where they are with the gifts of God.

2. This is a team effort.

Caring for young people in the church cannot be the responsibility of a single person. It must be a task shared with a variety of people, including parents and guardians, elders, pastors, and other volunteers. God works through all His people in a congregation to provide a community of believers to love teens and point them to Christ. As the Body of Christ, it's important that we share the responsibility for youth ministry. It is when God works through us together that we find a healthy youth ministry that cares for young people across time.

In developing your team, it is also important to bring a variety of people into load-bearing leadership roles. This should include youth and young adults as well as older, experienced leaders. A diverse set of skills is needed, too, from logistics and detail-oriented folks to those who are flexible and creative. A balanced team helps you connect with every youth and consider every part of ministry. Your team should also include your pastor(s), other staff, and key congregational leaders so they can support and champion youth ministry as well.

One of the things we hear most when we talk to people about the seven practices is that implementing them is either too much or too overwhelming. We don't want you to walk away from this book feeling as though every practice rests on your shoulders alone. The pressure of putting this all on yourself can crush you. Instead, bring teammates in along the way. Share this book and discuss it. Find people who see your goals and will help you set up a plan to get there. Know that every step in pointing young people to Jesus is God's doing as the Holy Spirit works through you.

3. This task is worth it.

We don't think you picked up this book if you don't think the task is worth it. Yes, faith is important at every age. Yes, we are a bit biased toward youth. But adolescence is a critical time for developing the understanding, resiliency, and vocations that will engage their faith in a lasting way. Young people are not the church of tomorrow; they are the church today. God has called these youth into His family through Baptism. Youth ministry with and for them can have a lasting impact today and for eternity.

It can be easy to look around your congregation and find fewer teens and young adults than you expect. The reality is that we have not retained the majority of the young people who start off in the LCMS for several generations now. We know from the LCMS's annual statistics that we currently retain 60–70 percent of our young people in the LCMS from Baptism to Confirmation. We retain around 34 percent of those from Confirmation into young adulthood. That means we retain around one in every five young people we baptize through to young adulthood.[1]

FIGURE 1: U.S. BIRTHS COMPARED TO PERCENTAGE BAPTIZED

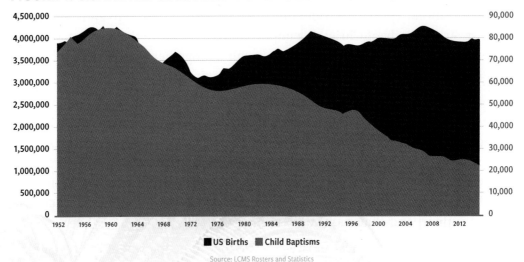

US Births   Child Baptisms

Source: LCMS Rosters and Statistics

FIGURE 2: RETENTION RATES

We have to be realistic about our retention rates.

60–70% from Baptism to Confirmation.

33% from Confirmation to young adulthood.

In the LCMS we retain 20% of those we baptize into adulthood.

1   LCMS Office of National Mission—Youth Ministry, *Relationships Count: Engaging and Retaining Millennials* (St. Louis: Concordia Publishing House, 2019), 26.

Every time we share those statistics, we lament. It never gets easier to say or share because it shouldn't be. Our struggles with retention aren't new. While the retention rate has decreased over time, Baptism rates were dropping in comparison to births in the United States as early as the baby boomers. This does—and should—break our hearts. Yet we cannot stay in a state of lament. With the power of the Holy Spirit, we turn to God's Word and the Christian community, and we strive to do better.

One way we change those statistics is by seeking to develop healthy youth ministry. We each play a role by embracing our vocations as parents, supportive adults, and congregational and youth ministry leaders. With God's help, we continue the work, even when we don't see how God is working and using us in a young person's life. God can and will continue to grow the seeds of faith He has planted through us. We don't always see the impacts we make. We can be encouraged to stick with youth ministry because, as stated before, none of this is a short-term quick fix.

4. This is about Jesus.

Jesus is at the heart of every single one of the seven practices. Without faith in Jesus, and His death and resurrection, nothing we do in youth ministry means anything at all. While youth ministry can be dramatically different from congregation to congregation, Jesus is the vital thing we all share. Youth ministry is designed to help young people to know Jesus and to live lives reflective of their faith in Him.

> JESUS IS AT THE HEART OF EVERY SINGLE ONE OF THE SEVEN PRACTICES. WITHOUT FAITH IN JESUS, AND HIS DEATH AND RESURRECTION, NOTHING WE DO IN YOUTH MINISTRY MEANS ANYTHING AT ALL.

In 1 Corinthians 15:14, we read, "And if Christ has not been raised, then our preaching is in vain and your faith is in vain." Without the salvation bestowed by Jesus' death and resurrection, everything else is just futile. Jesus has been raised, and in that, we have our hope. From community-building to Bible study, the cross and empty tomb should be at the center of everything we do. Healthy youth ministry should seek to point youth leaders, parents, and teens back to the love of Jesus and the forgiveness we receive through His death and resurrection.

Why the Seven Practices of Healthy Youth Ministry?

It happens in congregations around the country every year: the church leadership makes plans for a voters meeting where the new members of boards, committees, or other leadership teams will be elected. They prayerfully consider who to ask to step into the roles that help the church function, teach, and share the Gospel in its community. Maybe these spots fill easily; maybe they are a little more challenging to fill.

Youth ministry (or maybe it's called Christian education in your congregation) is often one of those groups that need additional leaders. It is a big and important task to care for the young people of our church, so perhaps someone steps up. Perhaps another is "volun-told." Parents want to make sure there are youth programs in the church for their children. Young adults who themselves experienced a safe, Christ-centered youth ministry in their teens want to ensure others have that as well. And so they are voted in for a term or two to help lead youth ministry.

We know that the majority of youth ministry in the LCMS is done by lay leaders. These passionate, capable, and thoughtful people volunteer their time to care for the teens of the congregation and community. Often, they are overwhelmed with responsibilities and do not have time to spend looking through the latest research or the ability to take time off work to pursue continuing education opportunities. Some congregations do have trained and called staff with responsibilities to youth ministry. However, they may also struggle with being pulled in many directions or helping volunteer leaders head toward a common vision.

We have a soft spot in our hearts for youth leaders, and it's our great joy to serve them well. Working with preteens and teens takes a special combination of gifts, skills, and passions. It's not for everyone. But when you find youth ministry is something you love, it gets ahold of you and doesn't often let go. As we travel around the country for different events, youth leaders—both professional and lay— are some of our favorite people to spend time with. It's not just their great stories, though they usually have a few. It is their love for Jesus and their love for sharing Jesus with youth.

The seven practices of healthy youth ministry were written with those youth leaders in mind. It was written to answer their questions and support their desire for healthy youth ministry. There were a few things that kept us from simply suggesting other resources that were already available.

In a recent survey we conducted, youth leaders reported that 39 percent of LCMS congregations regularly connect with between four and nine young people each month; 21 percent do not receive any budget for youth ministry outside of staffing or support for events like the LCMS Youth Gathering.[2] Not every congregation is going to have the same resources, whether in terms of people or money. Yet we have seen congregations get scrappy and creative, engaging in quality, Christ-centered youth ministry with next to nothing. Would more volunteers, resources, and teens be a blessing? Absolutely. Yet we wanted the seven practices to be reflective of the reality of youth ministry, not based on an imagined ideal.

Many mainstream youth ministry resources start with assumptions about staffing, budget, and facilities that are easy to use and access. Most of our congregations do not have a dedicated staff member or an overflowing budget. Other mainstream resources may suggest using small-group leaders as though every ministry has a huge number of teens and volunteers. In these resources, there may be little discussion of how to use confirmation programming or little value placed on intergenerational worship, which we emphasize. We wanted this book to reflect the more common makeup, staffing, and resources of churches in our denomination.

Every week, youth leaders flood search engines with searches for resources and direction. It can be difficult at best to sort through what to use with your young people. When searching online, you may find many helpful youth ministry books, blogs, and other resources that do not completely reflect the Lutheran understanding of discipleship. You may find that you are having to filter through pages and websites with a Lutheran lens. As you encounter the seven practices, we want them to plainly reflect our Lutheran theology with Lutheran congregations in mind. While we did not want to re-create the wheel, we did see that there was a lack of resources that aligned with our practices and understanding.

Youth ministry resources may also focus almost exclusively on youth programming and those who are dedicated solely to serving in youth ministry. This makes sense in many ways, but we find this emphasis leaves out key people and programs outside of youth ministry. While we do focus on youth ministry, you will find that we also often discuss the importance of supportive adults, service, and even leadership that happens outside of youth ministry programming. Youth ministry is

---

2   LCMS Youth Ministry, "Survey of Youth Leaders," August 2020.

a part of God's work in a congregation, and it shouldn't be separated or siloed apart from it.

Now when youth leaders reach out to us with questions about what congregational youth ministry should look like, we are excited and confident about our response. We share the seven practices of healthy youth ministry with them, and this book will share them with you too.

There will be aspects of the seven practices that will prompt even more questions. In fact, we included a series of questions after some of the chapters for you to think about and discuss as parents and leaders in your congregation. You can also answer these questions for yourself by digging into God's Word and listening well. How you answer them will help you continue to evaluate and guide your youth ministry. It is our hope that those questions and their answers will prompt small, consistent movement toward healthier youth ministry for your young people.

We want those leaders stepping into those roles to go in with humble confidence that God will work through them. The seven practices flow from the heart we have for youth leaders, professional or lay, who desire to build healthy congregational youth ministry. When you are a part of youth ministry, you are doing something vital for the church and for your teens. Thank you for dedicating your time and energy to the care of today's youth.

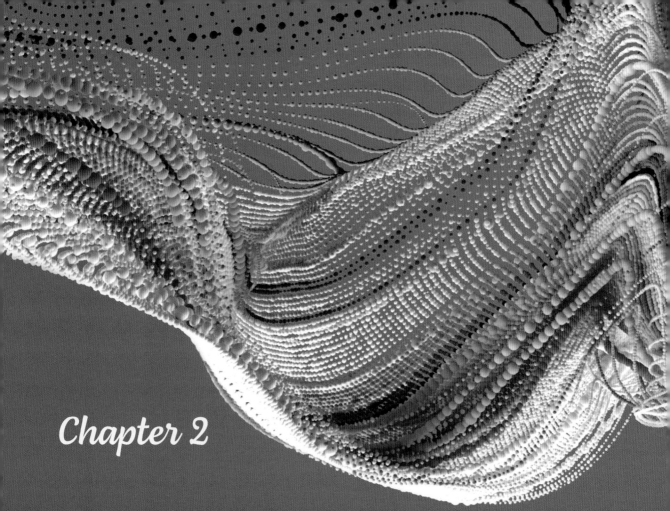

Chapter 2

CONGREGATIONS WITH HEALTHY YOUTH MINISTRY HAVE . . .

At least once a year, as we connect with districts and congregations, we get a question or joke about bringing back Walther League.

Julianna would hear this request to bring back Walther League regularly in the congregation she served. As a young DCE, it used to irritate her to no end. It felt like older adults were questioning her abilities as a youth leader or minimizing what her current youth ministry was doing.

After seminary, Mark became a member of a congregation with a rich Walther League history. When older, wiser adults found out he worked in the LCMS Youth Ministry office, people often mentioned that they should bring back Walther League. At first, he was flummoxed for a response. Later, he landed on a standard response: "Tell me why Walther League was so impactful in your life."

Over time, we began to see that it was less about the quality of our current ministry and more about the impact Walther League had on them in their formative teen and young adult years.

In the late 1800s, young Lutheran men and women began to form societies where they would gather to study God's Word and build one another up in Christian community. These groups developed over time into what we know as Walther League. Made up of those from around fifteen to thirty years old, Walther League included social activities, service, national conventions, and studying God's Word, all led by the young people themselves. While Walther League was an organization separate from the congregation, each chapter had to be supported by a local congregation.[3]

For many years, Walther League gathered young people under their five-fold program: worship, education, fellowship, service, and recreation. From the start, Walther League was led by young people elected by their peers into local and national leadership. As early as 1897, there were records of chapters serving their congregation and community from raising money to fix windows to sewing clothes for children who could not afford clothing. Walther League offered access to resources like a regular magazine, books, and connections to homes and jobs when they moved. All this helped deepen their understanding of their faith and their connection to the church. It shouldn't be surprising that some of those themes are still evident in the seven practices.

As you look at the history of Walther League, you cannot help but see

---

3   For more on Walther League, see Jon Pahl, *Hopes and Dreams of All: The International Walther League and Lutheran Youth in American Culture, 1893–1993* (Eugene, OR: Wipf and Stock, 2006).

commonalities shared with youth ministry today. There were questions about how to balance the need for social activities and community-building with time together in God's Word. Young people pressed boundaries of what older adults felt was appropriate behavior. Congregational leadership and parents worried about youth developing their own group within the church that disconnected them from the important intergenerational nature of worship and greater congregational life. Young people had disagreements. Youth tried to figure out how to live and find belonging in an ever-changing world with the lens of their Lutheran faith, while parents worried whether Walther League would help them keep their children in the faith. Some youth stepped into leadership roles, where some found success, while other youth only experienced struggles.

Youth ministry leaders, does any of that sound familiar?

God used programs like Walther League to impact the lives of many young people. Members of Walther League found a place that helped them understand their faith more deeply, develop lifelong relationships, and develop crucial leadership skills. It was also tied heavily to its time. You might be hard-pressed today to sell lapel buttons or raise money using Christmas seals. Eventually, changing times, controversy, and other struggles of this world meant an end to Walther League. But its history and example remain.

Since Walther League, there have been other models for youth ministry in the LCMS. Lutheran Youth Fellowship began in 1978 out of the LCMS Youth Ministry office. Originally designed as a national youth ministry network, it quickly refocused its work on training young leaders. Those leaders were sent and supported by their districts to train and care for young people closer to home. The LCMS Youth Ministry office developed a handbook to help youth ministries form boards and leadership groups of youth and adults to guide youth ministry. Some congregations still today call their youth ministry Lutheran Youth Fellowship (LYF). Over time, this highly structured way of training and networking became harder to maintain and the program had to shift. The training of teen leaders continues today as YouthLead, but it is open to both congregations and districts.

Other congregations have used programs and books to help guide the development of their youth ministry. Perhaps your ministry has sought to be "purpose-driven" or "simple." Models for youth ministry change as time goes by and the culture shifts. Congregations have served their young people in a variety of ways at different times. While the Word of God and what we teach do not change, the way we plan, engage, and program toward young people might. As new generations pass through our youth ministries, congregations may feel unprepared to face the unique gifts and challenges of working with teens today.

Looking back through history, we can see both commonality and difference in youth ministry. If you grew up in the church, you may look fondly back at your time in youth ministry. You may even want to re-create that for young people in your church. We want to avoid idealizing our youth ministry experience and leaving out the struggles. Instead, the seven practices may help us see more clearly where God worked powerfully through youth ministry. This helps us capture what we truly want to re-create for our young people.

For example, some of those who asked to go back to Walther League loved the games they played. However, I doubt that teens today are going to be quite as excited about a peanut hunt or square dancing as older adults might be. What may be more important to capture is what was valuable about those games. Was it a chance to be with peers and develop a community of friends who were Christians? Was it that the games helped take their mind off struggles at home or in the world and experience warmth and grace? Was it that the games were directed by youth and that they appreciated the chance to serve and lead? When we know why those games were so important, we can make choices that help to provide the same experience for youth today in a context that meets them where they are.

In every era, Jesus is proclaimed through Word and Sacraments. Regardless of what the programs or strategies looked like, youth ministry should always have Jesus at the center. Everything else is directed from there. Youth ministry needs to meet teens where they are today, in a time and culture that does not always support or see value in the Christian faith. We can learn from and retain what was valuable from past youth ministry. We can also learn lessons from the mistakes made in past youth ministry. Regardless of program or time, God has continued to use His people to serve teens and His Word to draw them closer to Him.

Practices for Congregations

The first four of the seven practices (Warmth, Challenge, and Grace; Supportive Adults; Engaged Parents; and Opportunities to Serve and Lead) are focused on the opportunities, people, and environment of the congregation and home. Rather than focusing on programs or networks, these concentrate on qualities each congregation can have.

Warmth, *challenge*, and *grace* are the words we use to describe the environment or culture of a healthy youth ministry. This can seem a bit hard to pin down, yet, at the core of it, God works in and through people and relationships to develop factors critical for faithful growth in God's Word. Healthy congregations have an environment that builds trust, fosters Christlike relationships, and helps weather the storm of teenage and young adult years. In contrast, an unhealthy culture can create animosity, frustration, hurt, and make it easier for young people to walk away.

Supportive adults are faithful Christians whom God has placed in the lives of young people to listen to them, pray for them, and cheer them on. These adults play a key role in caring for and discipling young people, especially as they begin to develop independence away from their families. God designed His family to include supportive adult relationships that can advocate for and champion young leaders as they walk through the good times and their struggles. God has blessed youth with many adults who can share their experiences, help support their faith practices, and encourage them to stay faithful. The investment in each youth by faithful Christian adults is powerful for congregations and youth ministry.

Parents are gifted with the role of primary instructors and set the example for their children in the Christian faith. While not every family looks the same, we know God can work in and through any person who takes on this critical role in a young person's life. Engaged parents model faith practices and teach Christ-centered priorities in the home. Engaged parents invest in the lives of their children by understanding their children's vocations and the culture around them. With such a critical role, youth ministry can work alongside parents, supporting and partnering with them, to the benefit of both parents and teens.

From Confirmation, many youth are considered adult members of the congregation and should be expected to take on roles of service and leadership. By identifying a teen's passions, gifts, and skills, youth ministry can help provide places where young people can serve effectively. Youth can be given opportunities to provide input and ideas toward ministry as well as chances to actively use their gifts. Some can be guided to mentors who will give them leadership roles. All of these things can provide a sense of ownership and positively impact the teen, congregation, and community.

Where Should We Start?

We have shifted the order of these practices over time. While we see each of them as important, it is hard to know what to focus on first. We know that engaged parents are the primary faith mentors in the lives of their children, but not every young person is blessed with two faithful parents. When we consider congregational youth ministry, we often find parents are partnering heavily with supportive adults to ensure youth ministry is discipling young people well. Warmth, challenge, and grace can seem difficult to create and maintain, but their presence or absence changes ministry dramatically.

As you can already see, each of these practices impacts the others. They are not separate but rather interlocking pieces. As you work to actively connect young people to supportive adults, you are encouraging the warmth, challenge, and grace that can come through those relationships. When you work with parents to understand each youth individually, you are more equipped to find opportunities to serve and lead where young people will be successful.

As you read through the next four chapters, we will outline each of the practices in more detail. Before you start to make an action plan with your next steps, be sure to read the whole way through. We know you might be encouraged to jump on "Warmth, Challenge, and Grace" before you look to opportunities to serve and lead. But you may find that your first idea for how to practice healthy youth ministry might not be the most impactful. Because the practices impact one another, once you have read them all, we hope you will find that there are strategic changes or actions you can take that give you a bigger impact because they have greater ripples beyond just one practice. C. F. W. Walther was the first LCMS president and the one for whom Walther League was named. He once reportedly said to his seminary students, "You cannot use your time to better advantage than by serving well the young people of the congregation." We pray your congregation believes this as well. While youth leaders have a variety of tasks and roles, one of them is reminding the congregation why youth ministry has value.

Teens are good at telling if the people around them truly have their best interests at heart. They sense all the big and little ways a congregation communicates young people's value to the church. Congregations that believe young people are important hear it communicated regularly by leadership and members alike. They will witness actions that encourage and value them. Young people will see their input invited and their gifts and skills celebrated. When a congregation values its youth ministry, young people see that in every aspect of the congregation.

Healthy youth ministry needs commitments of time, energy, and resources. It is hard to get that when, in small and large ways, other aspects of ministry dominate. It's important to infuse and reinforce the value of youth ministry to all members, both longtime and new. It can be easy for youth ministry to get lost or dismissed in times of difficulty, transition, or when there is simply a lack of young people regularly in your pews. Those who champion youth ministry can help keep its importance in the minds of members and leaders.

Reading this book can be a strong indication that your congregation believes youth are important. We, like you, believe that youth ministry is vital. We pray that God will work through your congregation to provide young people warmth, challenge, and grace; supportive adults; engaged parents; and service and leadership opportunities.

Chapter 3

WARMTH, CHALLENGE, AND GRACE

What words would you use to describe your congregation?

How would your youth describe your congregation?

How would young people in your community describe your congregation?

We look at many markers of success in youth ministry: worship attendance, program attendance, confirmation numbers, and retention rates through high school and beyond. We like tangible markers of success. It looks good to have numbers tracking upward for the voters meeting report. What we often don't track is the environment and culture of a youth ministry. This is a much hazier thing. However, if we aren't tracking, for lack of a better word, the "feel" of our youth ministry, we miss important indicators, both positive and negative.

As someone who likes the consistency and trackability of hard data, Julianna was a little hard to convince that the environment of youth ministry should be the first and, in some ways, overarching idea of the seven practices. There were two experiences that changed her mind.

First, when she moved to St. Louis, she found that for the first time in her life, she could attend a variety of churches before choosing the congregation where she would become a member. This freedom to explore felt delightful at the start. She was excited to experience the variety of churches in the area. In every worship service, she received God's good gifts, including the Sacrament of the Altar, which fed and sustained her in faith. She felt confident she could visit all kinds of new congregations because when we have what is most important, there is never a right or wrong answer.

What surprised her was how vastly different every congregation was, in some ways that were easy to identify and others that were harder to put her finger on. In some congregations, she felt immediately drawn in while others made her feel isolated despite being surrounded by people. That impression wasn't limited to the quality of the greeters. There were lots of considerations, large and small, which formed an impression over the course of a Sunday morning or two. She struggled to identify what she was looking for and how she felt when she visited a congregation.

She recalls how her enthusiasm quickly waned. She was overwhelmed and felt untethered. She could see so much more clearly how people could get lost as they went through this same search process. She understood just how much an environment could impact how a person stayed connected or became disconnected from faith and the church.

Julianna's second experience happened during our 2016–17 research on millennials and the LCMS. As a part of that study, we received responses from over two thousand young adults who had grown up in the LCMS. Some of those had remained active in the church, though others had left for other denominations or left the church entirely. As she read the responses to that survey, millennials repeatedly described their church's culture as much as its intentional actions. This continued through the focus groups.

Millennials were just as likely to describe an environment created by peers and leadership as they were a deliberate action or event. They noticed that small things that built over time either led them to deeper engagement or greater disconnect. They could feel people and relationships shift when they looked different, had a crisis, or pushed against norms. Some said that even peers dissuaded them from attending or prompted difficult spiritual conversations. Julianna was repeatedly reminded that practices and norms in the church are often caught, not taught.

In what was spoken or unspoken, these respondents experienced either love and support or rejection and isolation. In ministry, we never compromise the Gospel, even when it is a stumbling block to some. Yet these stories showed that our attitudes and approach could be the stumbling block that keeps young people from hearing God's Word.

Over time, even the most quantitatively minded among the Youth Ministry office staff were convinced that the most intangible things permeate everything else done in youth ministry. We analyzed our research and came up with many words that could describe environments that seemed to positively impact health and retention. We used words like *safe*, *authentic*, *welcoming*, *empathy*, and *value*, but none seemed quite right. Many of the words we found were full of cultural baggage that might lead to misunderstandings. Others did not indicate the right balance of Law and Gospel we knew was key.

In the end, we settled on the words *warmth*, *challenge*, and *grace*.

Warmth

Warmth is characterized by displaying Christ's love for all people and a personal invitation to be part of the community of believers. Everyone, from guest to longtime member, should be welcomed generously to worship and ministry programming. All baptized members should be consistently reminded and shown they are an important part of the Body of Christ. While this can look different from place to place, we often see it in simple things like calling teens by name, greeting them with a smile, and finding space to include them. It shows up when young people get what they need to live out their vocations inside the church and out.

> WARMTH IS CHARACTERIZED BY DISPLAYING CHRIST'S LOVE FOR ALL PEOPLE AND A PERSONAL INVITATION TO BE PART OF THE COMMUNITY OF BELIEVERS.

Warmth is shown when people across generations are known and want to know others. As teens navigate important parts of identity development, they need spaces where adults of all ages can genuinely get to know them and provide them support. Warmth comes when we show grace and encouragement every time a teen steps into the church. It happens when they are confident there is a seat for them and that others see them as God does. Warmth can't be performative or surface level. It must come from an outflow of the Gospel and the authenticity of our own forgiven hearts. Even those in the margins should feel it. Warmth values every young person we are called to serve.

Warmth allows for an open and honest environment where God's Word is spoken in love. Warmth doesn't mean we always have to be happy, perky, and optimistic. It comes from a deeper place that realizes that even in the most difficult times, we are brought together by God. We find warmth in belonging to the family of God where we receive God's forgiveness and love. In a warm environment, teens share their gifts and skills without fear that they will face ridicule or failure.

Warmth is a quality that we like to claim but we often don't deeply assess. It can be easy to assume that because we feel welcomed and cared for that others do as well. To assess warmth, we must put ourselves in the shoes of those less connected to our congregational community. When teens bring friends to church for the first time, they may have to navigate a minefield of unfamiliar norms and assumptions. It could be easy to bring judgment or to welcome too aggressively. Instead, we should focus on loving and welcoming others as Christ would do for us.

In one of Julianna's previous churches, there was a family who claimed that the back pew on the pulpit side belonged to their family. She had heard this jest in church before, usually at the expense of a visitor who sits where another family typically does. In this case, it wasn't just a joke. The family had been founding members of the congregation, and as such had donated to the building of the church. Consequently, they had received a gold plaque on a pew with their name on it.

The family matriarch once said that they had asked for their name to be on the very back pew. Why? Not because they were perpetually late or wanted to escape early for brunch. They had asked for this pew because it meant they could greet everyone. As leaders, it meant they could see who had attended and who might be missing. Visitors or folks who missed a few Sundays could count on the family to start a chain of conversations that made sure they were greeted and checked in on. They chose the last pew because they wanted to be sure everyone was welcomed and remembered. They wanted to build relationships that took the importance of warmth in community and worship seriously.

Challenge

Challenge can be used to describe two distinct characteristics: (1) willingness to approach difficult topics and situations, and (2) encouraging young people to step out in faith through the Holy Spirit, to be a light in dark places even when it is difficult. Both aspects of challenge are important to healthy youth ministry.

Standing firmly in God's Word, challenge means engaging young people in tough spiritual conversations. Teens encounter many voices every day, often speaking directly against what God says in Scripture. They need adults and peers who will face the questions and confusion in our current culture with them. Even when we feel we have taught them topics fully, it is important to take questions seriously. Challenging topics may need active listening and additional questions to get to the heart of the issue. Then, in response, we can spend time in God's Word, which can speak to even the most difficult issues.

FOSTERING CHALLENGE MEANS SETTING AN EXAMPLE FOR HOW YOU MAINTAIN RELATIONSHIPS WITH TEENS AND THEIR PARENTS WHILE ALSO BEING CLEAR ABOUT WHAT GOD SAYS IN SCRIPTURE.

One of the more difficult lines to walk as youth leaders is approaching young people who are in conflict or wrestling with sin. Even if they are not directly involved, teens are watching if we truly behave in a way that aligns with what we teach. They want to see what it looks like to address sin or conflict in love with the Gospel. Do we ourselves admit sin? Do we seek reconciliation with others when sin has broken a relationship? Challenge means that we do not let these things slide by. Instead, we take time to pray, talk, and speak the truth in love, even if that way is far messier.

Even the healthiest youth ministries are not immune to the impact of sin. There are many youth leaders who are navigating life with teens who are struggling with their sexuality or who are putting their priorities of achievement over their faith lives. Addressing these issues, and others like them, is never easy. Our sinful nature tempts us to avoid the difficult conversations or fail to address these topics in Bible study. Fostering challenge means setting an example for how you maintain relationships with teens and their parents while also being clear about what God says in Scripture. It never gets easier, but without the challenge of God's Law, unchecked and unrepentant sin can grow and lead to greater struggles down the road.

The second aspect of challenge means respecting young people as they are empowered by the Holy Spirit to live out their faith. Adults should use opportunities to challenge young disciples to actively engage in vocations, service, and leadership through the work of the Holy Spirit. Challenge does not underestimate young people. Instead, it gives them opportunities to grow, even if there is potential for failure.

Teens are learning to understand and grasp their gift of faith independent of family or other supportive adults. In doing so, they need opportunities to stretch what they know and how they share their faith. Challenge can mean encouraging teens to not compartmentalize or privatize their faith. Rather, challenge encourages them to find new ways to be God's hands and feet in the world. Challenging youth in this way isn't easy. In fact, you may worry that in pushing them you will alienate or ask too much of them. Yet you may find that youth want their faith to be so important that it demands their time, energy, and sacrifice. They want to know God will go with them and work in them when they stand up for what they believe. In challenge, we aren't afraid to tell teens there is nothing more important than faith in Jesus.

We will consider more about service and leadership in later practices, but challenge also includes letting youth take on service and leadership roles. This can be tricky as they learn and grow. Adult leaders may feel it is safer and more reliable to do it themselves. When you hold onto service and leadership for yourself, you take that challenge away from teens. Give them mentorship and support, but don't be afraid to challenge them, even if they fail. Offer them forgiveness and support when they do fail, and then find new ways to offer them a challenge again.

Grace

TEENS NEED TO BE CONSTANTLY REMINDED THAT THEIR CHIEF IDENTITY IS BEING GOD'S BELOVED BAPTIZED CHILD.

Grace in our relationships and culture echoes God's love and forgiveness to us. Teens are sinful humans who break relationships and fall for the temptations of this world. They are still learning, growing, and developing. As Christians, we meet these struggles differently than the world. We repent of sin and encourage others to repent when they are burdened by sin. We speak mercy, love, and forgiveness through Jesus Christ. Teens need to be constantly reminded that their chief identity is being God's beloved baptized child.

We fill an environment with grace not on our own but because of Jesus. This makes room for the Holy Spirit to step into difficult and trying situations. We speak words of confession and absolution often. In conversation, teens and adults should regularly share personal stories of grace, failure, challenge, and joy. This helps us see how God is at work in our lives. As young people struggle, they need a community of believers who support, teach, and share the Gospel with them, always reminding them of the God who sent His Son for us all.

First Corinthians 13:1–3 reminds us that we can say and do all the right things, but if we do it without the love of God, it is just "a noisy gong or a clanging cymbal." It is nothing. Paul calls the way of love a "still more excellent way" (1 Corinthians 12:31). It does not matter how precisely you run your many programs, whether or not your youth room is bright and filled with technology, or if you have the most engaging social media plan. Youth ministry is nothing but loud games and banging dodgeballs if it isn't rooted deeply in the love of Jesus Christ. If you try to do youth ministry without God's love, it is not worth anything. When we look at the qualities of love that Paul writes about in 1 Corinthians 13, we are reminded of how we should be toward one another and especially toward our young people. If you want to know what it looks like to bring warmth, challenge, and grace to your teens, this passage is a beautiful place to start.

We are going to fail when it comes to being kind, patient, and undemanding. On our own, we cannot bring grace to the teens in our community and congregation.

Yet Jesus was perfect and showed us immeasurable grace in His death on our behalf. God works these things as He ties people of all ages together in the congregation where we share in God's good gifts. As the Holy Spirit works, these qualities fill our relationships and our time together. As they do, we can continue to point young people to our salvation in Jesus, which has meaning now and throughout their lives.

Warmth, Challenge, and Grace in Practice

There is a lot to unpack in these three words. As we looked through Scripture and picked these three words to represent the first practice, we saw them exemplified over and over in the Gospels. One place we can look to is the story of Zacchaeus (of Sunday School song fame). In Luke 19, we read that Zacchaeus was the chief tax collector, and though it made him rich, it did not endear him to the people around him. In fact, Zacchaeus was seen as a traitor and a sinner, someone whom a "good" person of God would not be seen with. Yet, when Jesus arrived in Jericho, Zacchaeus wanted to see Him so badly that he was willing to climb a tree to get a better view.

When Jesus approached, He spotted Zacchaeus, looked at him, and spoke to him. We see warmth in action as Jesus saw this man in a tree and called him by name. But Jesus didn't stop there. Jesus invited Himself to stay with Zacchaeus, extending His warmth to the hospitality of a meal. Those in the crowd did not receive this well, especially those who may have been injured by this tax collector (or those like him) who now welcomed Jesus joyfully into his home. As we hear many times in the Bible, people grumbled about Jesus' actions.

We don't know all the details of the interaction that followed during the meal, but Zacchaeus was changed. Jesus challenged Zacchaeus's sin, and Zacchaeus repented—he didn't just give a cursory recognition that he may be a sinner. Instead, Zacchaeus committed to making things right with those he sinned against. Jesus' response was full of grace: "Today salvation has come to this house, since he also is a son of Abraham. For the Son of Man came to seek and to save the lost" (Luke 19:9–10). Not only was Zacchaeus's sin challenged but so was the judgmental sin of all those who grumbled. The grace of God wins in the end.

We see this even more in the Epistles. After our research, and as we worked on the seven practices, Mark found himself drawn to sections of the letters he often spent little time with. While we love to read the Epistles for the Lutheran doctrine, Mark would usually quickly skip over the openings and closings of the letters. As we did our research and started to put together the seven practices, however, Mark spent more time lingering on these greetings. The lists of names, greetings, and encouragements struck him differently. He found so much that was written reminded him of the value of relationships. These are people Paul loves. They are people to whom Paul preached the Word and toiled alongside—they even risked their safety for him.

As Paul wrote to the churches he founded or guided, he often wrote about the prayers he lifted up for them. He rejoiced in their joys, carried their burdens, and anguished over their sin and misuse of the Gospel. Prayer is powerful. In the universal church, local congregations, and family units, God invites us into deep prayer for one another. We give thanks to God for faithful parents and family members who share forgiveness and grace with young people. We pray for pastors, church workers, supportive adults, and youth themselves as they share their joys and trials together and impact lives with the Gospel of Jesus. We pray for the Holy Spirit to build in us fervent love, reflected in welcoming Christian communities where people of all ages walk together through the joys and challenges of living as Christians. In these interactions, we imitate the love of Jesus Christ, which makes all the difference in the life of those whom He claims in Baptism.

> AS WE LOOK TO DEVELOP WARMTH, CHALLENGE, AND GRACE IN OUR YOUTH MINISTRY, WE LOOK TO JESUS AS OUR PERFECT EXAMPLE. WE GIVE HOSPITALITY, HOPE, AND GRACE TO ALL THE YOUNG PEOPLE WE MEET. WE PRAY, AS PAUL DID, AS WE BUILD RELATIONSHIPS THAT SEE US THROUGH THE UPS AND DOWNS OF LIFE.

As we look to develop warmth, challenge, and grace in our youth ministry, we look to Jesus as our perfect example. We give hospitality, hope, and grace to all the young people we meet. We pray, as Paul did, as we build relationships that see us through the ups and downs of life.

In our research, we also identified some specific ways we know these relationships can be developed.

Congregations foster an open and honest environment where youth share joys, questions, crises, and doubts, knowing God's Word will be spoken in love.

Adolescence can be a tumultuous time of development. While you may remember your teen years fondly (or maybe not so fondly), you were also never a teen in today's culture.

The world is changing, and with it, our teens today will experience different questions, crises, and doubts than adults felt at that age. Fostering an open and honest environment means taking deliberate steps to ensure that youth know that they can approach supportive Christian adults, parents, and peers with anything on their minds.

One of the ways to foster this environment is to set an example of what it looks like when the Holy Spirit works through us to love others and live out our vocations. We can and should teach what God's Word says, and then live that out in our day-to-day relationships, roles, and responsibilities. Both as teens struggle and as they find success, they are watching us.

As leaders, we can share stories of how God is working in and through us when we teach. As we ask teens to consider how God's Word prompts them to respond in their lives, youth leaders should be answering this question of themselves as well. This can include sharing how God worked through difficult times in our past or how God is using us in new places to share the Gospel. We should think about the way we conduct our lives, our presence on social media, and our interactions with others—including youth—to ensure these match up with what we say is true in God's Word. When we are open and honest, our youth will be more comfortable doing so as well.

Congregational communities can be a teen's testing ground to see if the love described in God's Word is effectively applied and active in real life. Teens are developmentally working through stages where they test if what they have been taught really stands up to experience. The congregation may be the first place they go to see if we really do offer confession and absolution to one another when we hurt one another. They want to see if we truly welcome those who are different from us. Only Jesus will be the perfect model, but even in our sin, we can be honest about our mistakes and in asking forgiveness. The Holy Spirit working in the congregation can reflect the love of Jesus, always pointing to the cross as young people navigate joy and struggle.

The more we can show grace and openness in challenging and difficult circumstances, the more teens are going to be willing to share. An open and honest environment needs

ONLY JESUS WILL BE THE PERFECT MODEL, BUT EVEN IN OUR SIN, WE CAN BE HONEST ABOUT OUR MISTAKES AND IN ASKING FORGIVENESS. THE HOLY SPIRIT WORKING IN THE CONGREGATION CAN REFLECT THE LOVE OF JESUS, ALWAYS POINTING TO THE CROSS AS YOUNG PEOPLE NAVIGATE JOY AND STRUGGLE.

mutual trust and respect—which is built over time. It is not something we can simply declare or put on a few posters and assume young people will share what is going on in their lives and hearts. It's also something that can be easily lost. We build this environment over time in our responses and actions when joys, questions, challenges, and doubts come.

If we want young people to be challenged in a positive way to stretch beyond their comfort zone, then we should be willing to be there when things don't go as expected. Young people are often terrified of what may happen if they try and fail. The church can be a place where failure is not avoided but met with grace and forgiveness. In a world that is looking for perfection and is ready to cancel those who make mistakes, the church may be one unique place where they can try, fail, and find forgiveness and restoration. In fact, we know that as we seek to share the Gospel, God may even do far more through us and young people than we could ever imagine.

One thing you can count on in youth ministry is crisis and doubt. Youth leaders should be prepared for this inevitability, no matter how steady the young person and their family. As young people become independent, we can expect they are going to ask hard questions about what they have learned about their baptismal faith. When that crisis, doubt, or struggle occurs, we want young people to look to God's Word and lean in to their baptismal identity. An environment of warmth, challenge, and grace is formed when we teach youth there are no questions too difficult for our faith to face. Even more, we can teach that we go together to God's Word and Sacraments, leaning on one another when doubts come and our youth see sin and darkness in the world.

There was a time when if we had questions about faith, we were dependent on books, pastors, or adults with advanced learning. Now, information is available in an instant online. The information at our youths' fingertips may come from many sources, including ones that are untrustworthy or unbiblical. Now, our role as youth ministry leaders has shifted to helping them use Scripture as a lens for understanding the information they find. We need to set an example and teach them how to find solid biblical answers to questions. As they walk through difficult times, we can help them filter what they hear and see through God's Word for us.

One word of caution: open and honest doesn't mean that adults should share without boundaries. It is important for teens to hear how the adults around them have struggled and been forgiven and enlightened by the Holy Spirit. What we don't want is for adults to overshare with teens or to feel like they should share every personal story they have. The youth in your congregation are not your friends in the same way your peers are. There should always be checks and balances that make sure that healthy relationships are maintained even as we walk with teens in difficult times.

Congregations share personal stories of grace, failure, challenge, and joy.

God intended us to be people who share stories, particularly stories of God's good gifts and work. In Joshua 3–4, the Israelites were finally being led into the Promised Land after forty years in the desert. The ark of the covenant was brought into the Jordan River and God performed a miracle allowing all His people to pass across the waterway on dry land. Once all the Israelites had passed, God gave the instruction for every tribe to send someone to the middle of where the Jordan was parted and take up a stone. These stones were carried to where they rested that night. On the face of it, these seem like curious instructions, but God had a specific purpose for these stones.

Joshua set up these stones, which the day before were at the bottom of a moving river, on dry land. He then told the people that these stones were set up so that when future generations ask what they mean, they could point them back to the moment when God acted to save them and bring them to the Promised Land. God wanted a physical reminder that would give opportunities for many generations to tell the story of God's salvation. Perhaps we don't have a pile of rocks today, but we still have things around us that serve to jump-start important narratives about God's work in our lives.

This is why Julianna always keeps a small photo of herself from middle school in her office. It is a good reminder to both her and her youth that she has not always been an adult with the knowledge and experience she has now. Aside from being good for a laugh, it sparks stories that help her point to things like her own confirmation journey and to the ways God used her youth ministry to form her.

Stories are powerful. Mark recalls being reminded of the power of telling a story, even to "those who know it best" and "seem hungering and thirsting to hear it like the rest."[4] In a recent visit to a church, Mark found they had a unique way of telling stories. Essentially, members were asked to (sometimes anonymously) place snippets of paper on a bulletin board with stories about how the Gospel had

---

4   "I Love to Tell the Story," stanza 4, public domain.

recently impacted their life. There were incredibly powerful answers. One person had made a bold move to try to reconcile with a family member. A young person was led to identify another student in their class who was lonely and just needed someone to notice them and be kind. Another student asked the Holy Spirit to protect him from ongoing temptation and sin. Mark was encouraged by the Holy Spirit just reading those stories. He can't imagine the impact for members to read how God was working in the lives of fellow members.

As the church, we hear the stories of God's deliverance in Scripture spoken in worship and studied personally and in community. Pastors preach Law and Gospel, retelling the story of salvation to the saints and reassuring them of Jesus' promises. Our God and His powerful Word are still at work in the lives of His people. The Word brings people into God's family, softens hard hearts, calls people to repentance, and refreshes them with the Gospel of Jesus. Just as people of old in the Bible told and retold stories of their deliverance (see Exodus 15, Psalm 78, Psalm 114), we tell of the story of our deliverance in Jesus. We get to tell the stories of the ongoing impact of God's acts of deliverance and grace.

Mentoring and reverse-mentoring can also set a stage for healthy youth ministry. Young and old can share their stories with one another to find points of connection and support. These stories can also be ways to share the history of a congregation to help young people see how God has used the congregation in their community and beyond. Personal narratives can be a powerful way for congregations to share warmth, challenge, and grace.

Congregations are willing to engage in tough spiritual conversations.

Nearly all youth leaders have had that moment—you are in the middle of your carefully planned Bible study. Your youth are engaged in the lesson, and suddenly, one of them has an incredibly difficult theological question. If you are lucky, it is on topic. If not, it threatens to take your time in a very different direction. When you are developing warmth, challenge, and grace, your response in this moment can be powerful.

When the difficult question is asked, is it met with disregard (or even frustration), or is it met with genuine interest and concern? In the 2019 Youth Poll at the LCMS Youth Gathering, one in seven young people who said LGBTQ issues were important to discuss also said they were unsure of their own view. In fact, we have seen an increase in this study over time of young people responding "I don't know" to questions of difficult social issues. In that same study, the top six issues teens listed as concerning them about their life and the world included abortion, mental health, gun control, their future, suicide, and reaching unbelievers. They want us to challenge them with difficult conversation.

Healthy youth ministry means making sure that youth know there is no question too difficult or simple for us to consider when it comes to faith in Jesus. When it is time to ask a challenging question, youth are going to be on edge and intensely aware if others show disapproval or frustration toward them. They are looking to be sure that if they push or stumble, the church will still show them the grace and love Scripture promises them. We look to impart the depth of our theology and our struggles as humans without filters or shallow fakery. When we do this well, we teach young people to come to God's Word, trusting that we can always find new things to learn about who God is and what God does for us.

Tough spiritual conversations should be done in partnership with parents and guardians. As the primary faith leaders of their youth, they need to be involved in these difficult conversations. Congregations and parents can work together to ensure there are many avenues they can address the topics they most want to know about.

In our Millennials and the LCMS study, we found that those who stayed active in the LCMS reported higher rates of believing their congregation handled conflict well and were more comfortable inviting friends to their home church than those who had left the church entirely. While it might be uncomfortable and we will certainly make mistakes, tough spiritual conversations are worth having often. They give space of warmth, challenge, and grace as young people sort out how to live their faith in a culture that does not support their Christian belief.

Congregations have a dedicated, developmentally appropriate space for youth where they grow as disciples with their peers.

Youth ministry is different than youth group. We may use the words interchangeably, but they indicate different intents. One is to care for young people in the congregation in whatever way we can. The other is tied specifically to programming for teens and preteens. We use the broader term *youth ministry* far more often, especially in situations where *youth group* can come with programmatic baggage. Yet there is an important place for youth group—where peers can experience time together in prayer, God's Word, play, and service.

One way to foster an environment of warmth, challenge, and grace is to have a dedicated space for youth where they grow as disciples with their peers. While healthy youth ministry is integrated into the larger congregation, there is a need for space, time, and resources specifically for young people. Yes, we want to have intergenerational components to our youth ministry. Also, yes, there is a need for age-specific ministry where teens can be together with one another in their own space.

Space here can mean a variety of things. The space we created can be digital or physical, permanent or temporary. While some congregations have facilities that allow for rooms that are specifically for teens, others may need to create that space in more creative, flexible ways. This space might even change over time. One of Julianna's congregations had a youth room, but its layout didn't really allow for good small-group conversation. So, for over a year, the Sunday night Bible study met at a local restaurant. For that time, youth ministry space was created in the middle of a busy eatery as the youth leaders talked, studied, and pointed young people to Jesus.

The biggest thing we can do is create space where adults can teach at a developmentally appropriate level and focus on the unique needs and questions of teens. Adolescence is a time when young students are asking critical questions about identity and belonging. They are trying on new pieces of identity to see what fits and discovering their gifts, skills, and passions. In the middle of these discoveries, they are working toward independence and making their own decisions. They are in stages where they are learning to form arguments and being introduced to new vocations.

There are entire books dedicated to the developmental stages that happen in adolescence. The more important point is that middle school and high school students need time to wrestle with some of the issues unique to this age with peers. Youth leaders need to advocate for them to find spaces where they can scripturally address issues of identity, belonging, and freedom with other Christian teens. That may mean youth leaders seek out other churches or even within their district resources to find places to connect. It may mean advocating for space, time, and money where teens can be together.

As we create these developmentally appropriate spaces, we need to be aware of how we support the faith lives of youth as they transition in and out of these spaces. They cannot be so separate from the larger church and its programs that young people drop away in those transitional moments. Instead, healthy youth ministry helps transition young people into its ministry and back out again eventually with supports, continued communication, and relational connections.

Warmth, Challenge, and Grace: Small Changes Consistently over Time

"Death by a thousand cuts." That was how one person described why he or she left the church after growing up in the LCMS. That phrase still sticks out years later because it encapsulates the experience that we hear from many who grow up in the church and walk away. This is one of the reasons why fostering warmth, challenge, and grace in your youth ministry is so important.

When we do not pay attention to the environment or culture of a church, we create a place where small cuts can go untreated. They fester and build on one another until it becomes less painful to leave the church than it is to stay. This environment is often not created maliciously but out of inattention. Youth leaders, professional or lay, are stretched too thin and serve in a spiritual, emotional, and resource deficit. They are gifted and well-intentioned, but between running from program to program, trying to communicate with busy families, and recruiting other volunteers, they don't have enough time. They simply let the climate of the youth ministry remain what it is.

An environment of warmth, challenge, and grace can bring balm to the ways, big and little, that we hurt one another. We can offer confession and absolution to one another. We can call out hurt without fearing retaliation or disregard. While the church will still be filled with sinful people, deliberate and specific action can be taken through the power of the Holy Spirit to slow and heal the injuries we cause to one another. God can and does work through us to make a space in our churches where young people find such community and encouragement that the thought of leaving is painful.

One of the pitfalls of talking about environment is that often it feels different to highly engaged, longtime leaders than it does to those who are closer to the margins. As you look to make small changes, one of the first things you can do is be aware of what actions you currently take that might be impacting ministry. It can be natural to spend more time and attention on the teens you know best, but that often leaves other teens disconnected. Maybe you use words or terms that not everyone is familiar with. Perhaps you get so focused on the activity of youth ministry that you lose the goal of pointing young people to Jesus. Don't let your need to get the pizza keep you from having important times of joy and connection with teens.

The changing of an environment or culture does not happen overnight, though many have tried. It cannot be forced. It starts with the work of the Holy Spirit as we make small choices over and over that reinforce warmth, challenge, and grace. Some of those small changes can include these:

- Praying often for the youth of your congregation and their families

- Calling young people by name

- Recruiting other adults to be consistently in communication with youth; this ensures that every teen has someone who is checking in and showing care for them

- Taking time during programming to listen well, even if that means you don't do everything you had planned (sometimes taking time to ask good questions and really listen allows you to speak God's Word in powerful ways, perhaps even more than the lesson you planned)

- Writing a note of encouragement or sending a text of support to teens experiencing stress

- Planning to talk about difficult topics—which may mean finding additional adults, like your pastor, to lead or doing extra work to prepare

- Celebrating together, even if it is small things—don't miss out on opportunities to rejoice in how God is using young people in their daily lives

- Apologizing when you do something wrong; it can be easy to just move on when you make a mistake, but the more often youth hear you ask for forgiveness and receive absolution, the more they will feel encouraged to do the same

- Bringing in older adults to share their stories and help find points of connection

- Taking time to learn about adolescent development and how parents and adults can help provide space for teens to learn and grow through these times

- Preparing for crises by making sure you have access to resources and professionals with which and to whom you can connect teens and their families

This can feel like just another list of things to do. Remember that God works in and through us so that consistent, small, deliberate changes can be powerful in their impact. They help form the culture and environment where the Gospel can be clearly shared and young people can be discipled well. As a leader, your words and actions set a tone whether you want them to or not. Considering how you can add even just one of these things can help move you closer to reflecting God's warmth, challenge, and grace.

Developing a culture of warmth, challenge, and grace means learning to be people of warmth, challenge, and grace through the work of the Holy Spirit. In these steps, we are not only setting an example but we are teaching young people how to bring warmth, challenge, and grace into their lives and vocations. We can teach these concepts, but it is all the more powerful when young people see them at work in our actions.

> DEVELOPING A CULTURE OF WARMTH, CHALLENGE, AND GRACE MEANS LEARNING TO BE PEOPLE OF WARMTH, CHALLENGE, AND GRACE THROUGH THE WORK OF THE HOLY SPIRIT.

We know that some young people feel the church is pushing them away one small cut at a time. At the same time, we heard from many youth who could not point to a single person or moment that drew them closer to Jesus and their church. Instead, they spoke about the many people and circumstances that built them up through small interactions—parents, extended family, supportive adults, peers, and congregations that gave them space to learn, grow, and serve. Instead of a thousand cuts, they experienced a great cloud of witnesses that pointed them regularly back to the cross and their gift of faith.

Every congregation has its own history, norms, practices, and community that all impact the congregational environment. We at the Youth Ministry office recognize the powerful factors that brought the church to where it is today while also seeing new possibilities of being in community together. We celebrate alongside the many people who grew up in the church and can point to a thousand different ways they have been cared for within the church. This life together in healthy congregations is where we believe healthy youth ministry happens.

There is no prescription or program for creating a healthy environment. We wish there was. Instead, the work of creating this environment of warmth, challenge, and grace is done by God through us over time, deep below the surface. The words we would use to describe our congregation may change over time as we integrate into the community and as congregations and leadership change. This means that the culture and environment can be impacted by our actions.

One of the most powerful things you can do is consistently make small, deliberate changes that will help form the culture and environment you want for your youth ministry. By taking small steps, leaders model God's love overflowing in action and build connections that share the Gospel. May God use you and many others to walk alongside teens and point them to Jesus with warmth, challenge, and grace.

DISCUSSION QUESTIONS

1. How would you, your youth, and your community describe your church?

2. Looking back, what is a time when and place where you felt warmth, challenge, and grace? What created that environment and how did it impact you and your experience?

3. How are you preparing youth leaders and parents for transitions, crises, and doubts?

4. What tough spiritual conversation have you engaged youth in lately? How might you prompt some of those conversations?

5. What space is available for your youth where they can be with their peers? How might we grow and enhance this space?

6. What are some small steps you might take to help develop an environment of warmth, challenge, and grace?

Chapter 4
SUPPORTIVE ADULTS

Not all of us remember our teen years fondly. Some of us avoid thinking about middle school and high school as much as possible. But just for a moment, think back on the adults who were with you during that time. Were there adults aside from your parents who listened to you and cheered you on? Were there adults who taught you about Jesus and who prayed for you? Were there adults who took a chance on you, even when you had not earned it?

Hopefully, you can remember adults in your life who made a lasting impact on you. As you look back, you may be able to see with new eyes just how powerful their presence was. Now you have a chance to be that same kind of adult for other young people. If you didn't have that kind of adult, perhaps now you want to support youth in a way you wish you were supported. In *Seven Practices of Healthy Youth Ministry*, we call these supportive adults.

God created and designed us for community, to be parts of the same Body of Christ. In Baptism, God brings people into His family—a family full of supportive adults of many generations. Those who witness the rite of Holy Baptism (likely our parents, godparents, and extended family but also a whole congregation) pray together for the baptized in this rite. They pray for God to help them guide, model, and teach the baptized person about who God is for us. They pray that person knows these adults only want God's best for them. The Holy Spirit works through many relationships as we walk through life to help shape us into who God made us to be.

While parents or guardians may be the most critical people in a youth's faith life, other supportive Christian adults can play a significant role in walking alongside youth in their faith development. Our research found that 72 percent of active LCMS millennials who grew up in the church and stayed said they had a safe person to talk to at church. Only 36 percent of those who grew up in the LCMS but are now unaffiliated with any church said the same. These faithful adults can come from just about anywhere. Supportive adult influence can come specifically through youth ministry, through other programs in the congregation, or through regular, organic interaction in worship.

Our research also found that the way young people were connected to and saw their home congregation made a dramatic difference. For example, when asked if they agreed that their home church supported their faith, only 39 percent of those who left the church agreed while 70 percent of those still active in the LCMS agreed. Similarly, when asked if their home church looked out for their best interest, only 18 percent of those who left the church agreed while 57 percent of those who were still active in the LCMS agreed. Supportive adults are one key way that young people feel their faith is supported by the congregation. This is part of why it is so important to find and engage supportive adults.

FIGURE 3: IMPACT OF HOME CHURCH EXPERIENCES
Young adults who identify as LCMS Lutherans (and especially those who are active) have more favorable views of their home church.

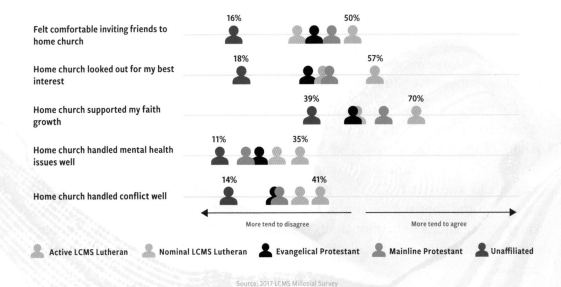

Source: 2017 LCMS Millenial Survey

Supportive congregations seek to connect every youth with at least five engaged Christian adults.

When we talk about risk management in youth ministry, we often talk about wanting at least one adult for every four to six youth. This ensures that you don't lose teens in a corn maze and can appropriately handle a medical emergency. Those are good rules to have. But when it comes to finding supportive adults, we want to flip this on its head.

We believe that every teen should have five supportive Christian adults in their lives. This is a number first suggested by Fuller Youth Institute in its book *Sticky Faith*.[5] In some cases, youth may have many of these adults, including extended family, Christian teachers, coaches, and youth ministry leaders. In other cases,

---

5   Kara Eckmann Powell and Chap Clark, "Sticky Web of Relationships," in *Sticky Faith: Everyday Ideas to Build Lasting Faith in Your Kids* (Grand Rapids, MI: Zondervan, 2011), 101.

teens may not interact with any adults who are providing them with support that points them to Jesus. When trying to meet this number, we don't count just any adult in their lives; supportive adults take on specific and important qualities.

Supportive adults

- **Ask good questions and provide a listening ear on everyday easy topics as well as difficult moments of struggle. Engaging in conversation is the place where we learn about one another.**

- **Share who they are in Christ, openly and honestly. This means showing both how God is working through them in their various vocations but also the ways in which they are still learning or struggling. In this space, they need to show challenge, but not judgment or critique.**

- **Set an example for teens by spending regular time in God's Word, prayer, and worship, and frequently use words of confession and absolution in their relationship. Supportive adults do not have to be perfect, but they are best able to point young people to Jesus when they are deeply rooted in Christ.**

- **Build a reciprocal relationship with mutual trust. This means having both a genuine interest in getting to know a young person including his or her gifts, skills, and passions but also a willingness to earn the right to be heard.**

- **Extend hospitality in sharing time, celebrations, joy, crises, and struggles as they walk alongside young people.**

Nearly every Christian adult can serve as a supportive adult to a teen. Sometimes those connections are made organically and other times they are developed through participating in programs. Older adults may connect to teens through service—altar guild, ushering, and VBS, for example. Adults can form connections with teens through their parents or even by sitting close to them in church each Sunday. Some congregations have specific

NEARLY EVERY CHRISTIAN ADULT CAN SERVE AS A SUPPORTIVE ADULT TO A TEEN programs for confirmation mentors. Others facilitate this by allowing Sunday School teachers to age up with a specific group of students. Regardless of how the connection is formed, being a supportive adult does not need to be complex or time-consuming.

Being a supportive adult isn't a one-way street. Adults should see this as less of a service and more of a strong relationship they build with teens. Teens have a lot of wonderful gifts that they bring to the relationship as well. They have a unique perspective and passion that is often lost in adulthood. As digital natives, they can bring a lot of insight into our culture today for those who grew up before cell phones. Each teen has gifts, skills, passions, and experiences that can be shared with mutual trust and honesty.

It is important to note that no pastor or other church worker can be the only supportive adult to all a congregation's teens. In order to be most effective, adults should limit the number of teens they are spending dedicated time supporting. Often, church workers are the people who are in a supportive relationship with every teen. Their time may instead be better served networking teens and adults through common passions, service, and programming. Remember, youth ministry is always a team effort.

When looking for supportive adults, it is critical that they are Christians who are active in learning about who God is and what Jesus Christ has done as well as in service and leadership. What they model, say, and do can have a tremendous impact. As God works through their vocations, supportive adults model and encourage faithful worship, Bible study, and prayer. In all they do, they should seek to draw young people closer to Jesus and to His church. Through good times and bad, supportive adults help keep God's Word in front of young people and show they have their eternal best interest at heart.

Supportive adults deliberately invest and value long-term, intergenerational relationships.

Youth ministry volunteers may find the first few steps of developing relationships with teens somewhat awkward. Life stage, experience, and even vocabulary differences might make it hard to instantly connect. You need to be ready to embarrass yourself a little in the process. Don't worry too much, though—those first few miscommunications and honest mistakes often help create spaces of mutuality and honesty. Simply be who God made you to be and enjoy who God made the teens in your congregation to be as well.

Finding supportive adults can be difficult, so it is important that you cast a wide net. The more broadly you talk about the need for supportive adults and what that means, the easier it may be to find them. It also helps when you expand your idea of who might be a supportive adult. When young adults to retirees are brought into greater involvement in supporting teens, we can utilize strengths from each generation.

God designed the church to be intergenerational. Teens especially benefit from being with a variety of ages. Young adults can relate to the world of teens. Teens are also more quickly able to picture their futures when they look to young adults who are modeling their vocations. Supportive adults who are of similar ages to a teen's parents (often other teens' parents) can be strong bridges between parent and teen, supporting both and helping ease communication. Older adults bring a wealth of experience and joy to young people. Often this is a space where mentoring and reverse-mentoring work best.

Like all relationships, it is okay to give it time to mature. Youth ministry leaders can ease that initial pairing by using opportunities for directed conversation or shared activity. Give them something to do together, like a strategy game or cooking a meal. Find topics of conversation that don't require intense personal disclosure. For example, youth and mentors in a confirmation program could be given discussion guides to help keep conversation flowing. In a first meeting between them, youth and mentors could go on a five-minute walk around the church campus to identify all the things they see, smell, and feel. When they come back, they could create a list together to start a lesson on the First Article. In examples like this, it's important to encourage adults to be as participatory as possible because it can help give solid footing to developing relationships.

Adults can have a meaningful impact on teens during a short season. However, long-term relationships are uniquely equipped to engage and reengage youth during transition and crisis. We found in our 2016–17 research on millennials in the church that when the leader (primarily pastors) reporting the retention rates of their confirmands had been around in the years between a given confirmation class and the report, there was better retention in the LCMS, as well as a lower instance (25 percent versus 43 percent) of the response "whereabouts unknown."

FIGURE 4: IMPACT OF PASTORAL LONGEVITY

There was a significant improvement in retention when pastors had been in their congregation during the time their confirmands grew into young adults.

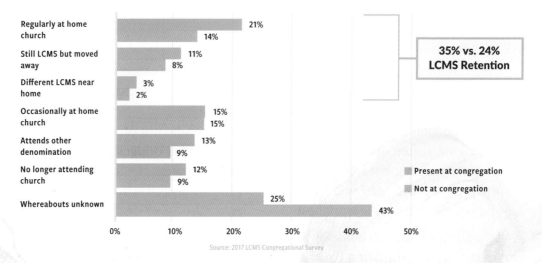

Source: 2017 LCMS Congregational Survey

What we can see here is that when leaders were around for longer periods of time, they were better able to retain youth into young adulthood and were better able to track youth people from confirmation to young adulthood.

Long-term relationships are powerful for several reasons. First, they can better keep connections with teens on the margins. With every leadership transition, those less connected are at increased risk of getting lost. When a lay leader or church worker is around for longer, they are better able to stay connected and reach out to those who may otherwise disconnect from the church. Second, long-term relationships are also a place where Law and Gospel can be spoken at appropriate times. The length of the relationship gives extra insight to determine when you need to speak God's Law or grace. Finally, they can build up the kind of mutual trust that gives young people the right to be heard. This is especially important for a generation of teens who have many voices telling them what to think on social media every day.

While some youth ministry leaders feel as though the youth are "tired of them" because they have led for years, there is an incredible value invested in those relationships. As we consider what is best for youth ministry, perhaps we should rethink how we place volunteers to be with a group or class over time. It can also cause us to change how we keep youth leaders connected even after they have stepped away from active ministry. It could be transformative if leaders were willing to think of themselves not just as drivers or chaperones but as long-term adults who are willing to engage a few young people deeply.

Supportive adults prepare for and respond to celebrations, transitions, and crises.

Adolescence is a time of ups and downs and big emotions. Teens need a community of peers, parents, and adults who will be with them through it all. Supportive adults help ground young people in their identity in Christ as they prepare for and respond to celebrations, transitions, and crises. As Romans 12:15 says, "Rejoice with those who rejoice, weep with those who weep." Supportive adults are uniquely set up to anticipate transition, spot rising issues, and engage at critical moments.

Being present for a student's celebrations is a joy. It does take some time and attention to do so. It can be helpful to keep a record of the sports and activities teens are involved in. If you can regularly ask for schedules to attend these events, you may find lots of options to cheer youth on. It also helps to pay attention when you talk to youth for small celebrations. It's just as important to recognize when a youth aces a test in a difficult class as it is for you to celebrate winning championship games. Big and small, when you rejoice with teens, they are reminded you have their best interests at heart.

It can be hard to talk about, but it is important to prepare for transitions and struggles. We can get ahead of those moments to allow us to be calm and present for teens in the moment. Knowing of valuable resources, encouraging timely conversations, and keeping communication open can all be powerful tools that God uses to keep youth in the community of faith. For example, supportive adults can plan to check in frequently on students who change schools, start a new job, or face family-dynamic changes. Youth leaders can also think through where they might suggest a parent can seek out professional counseling or books on difficult topics that can be shared. It can be helpful to take trainings like Mental Health First Aid[6] to grow in confidence in addressing mental health crises.

The need for supportive adults does not change as young people transition into college. In fact, their need may grow as they leave home and are stretched in new and unusual ways. This is the moment we most see young people leave the church (and few return), yet it is also a critical moment that supportive adults can prepare for. Supportive adults should be equipped to keep up communication and prayer

6   For more information, see Mental Health First Aid® from National Council for Mental Wellbeing, http://www.mentalhealthfirstaid.org.

as youth transition out of high school and into what comes next. Checking in regularly and helping connect them to new congregations or campus ministry helps ease this critical transition.

FIGURE 5: YOUNG ADULTS ARE MINISTERED TO BY THEIR HOME CHURCH DURING LIFE TRANSITIONS

Young adults are more likely to remain active in the LCMS when their home church stays connected with them during life transitions.

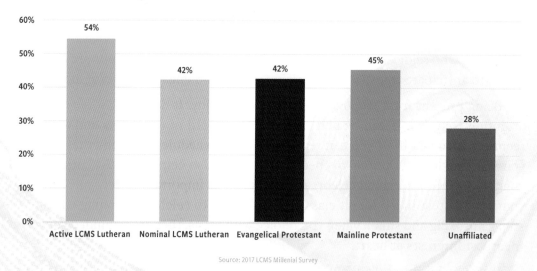

Source: 2017 LCMS Millenial Survey

Responding to a crisis is significantly harder since crises are difficult to prepare for. No matter how much planning and research you do, you will never quite feel ready. In those moments, we lean more on the work of the Holy Spirit and trust in His guidance. We know that being present at these key times helps young people know the adults God has placed around them are there for the lows as well as the highs. Through the Holy Spirit, these adults can pray for young people, be a loving presence, and continue to show up in whatever way that young person needs.

It can be easy to think in moments of shifting or struggle that the adult needs to have all the answers. God has given us His Word, on which we can stand firm. As we do, we know youth may still have difficult questions about life and faith. Adults should be honest about what we know to be true and where we still experience the mysteries of God. Teens want someone to be available to walk with them, pointing to the cross through joyful celebration, through times of change, and in difficult spots.

To properly walk with young people amid their own suffering demands that we, too, engage in our own brokenness. There are times when the crisis of a teen can hit a bit too close to home for an adult. It's important that if you are walking alongside a teen who is struggling, you also pay attention to how their struggle is impacting you. There may be moments where you need to defer to other adults and professionals, or simply identify ways you can keep your own balance and boundaries.

Supportive congregations have adults who champion young people and dedicate time and energy to developing teens as disciples of Jesus Christ for life.

Supportive congregations include special adults who are passionate about caring for the young people in their congregation and are willing to advocate for them. These youth leaders dedicate their time and energy to ensuring young people have the place and space to grow as disciples for life.

If you are looking for the champions of youth in your congregation, you can ask a few key questions to locate them:

- **Who is planning age-appropriate events for teens?**

- **Who is connecting young people with leadership opportunities?**

- **Who is advocating for resources for youth ministry?**

- **Who is getting them to district youth gatherings, LCMS Youth Gatherings, and other events?**

There are times when these youth leaders hold seats on youth boards or serve on the staff. Other times they have other leadership roles, like elder or church council member, but continually advocate for the resourcing and support of young people.

It is important that congregations identify these champions and encourage them. Thank them publicly and privately for their important work. If it is possible, provide them with resources and training so they can better know how to care for teens. Help them engage with other areas of church ministry and ask for their insight into important congregational decisions. The more supported these champions are, the more likely they will be able to serve long-term, which we know has a powerful retaining impact.

Okay, but What If . . .

One of the questions Julianna gets from adults most often when she talks about supportive adults is how to get to know teens without coming across as "creepy" or "weird." Adults worry that if they approach teens at random in their church narthex, their intentions will be mistaken and it will do more harm than good. This question comes from a good heart that wants to protect young people. It also comes a bit from our own insecurities as adults.

SUPPORTIVE ADULTS HOLD A UNIQUE PLACE WHERE THEY CAN CHEER YOUNG PEOPLE ON, LISTEN TO THEM WELL, AND MENTOR THEM. THIS RELATIONSHIP, HOWEVER, LIKE ALL IMPORTANT RELATIONSHIPS, MUST COME WITH CLEAR BOUNDARIES.

The priority of supportive adults, parents, and congregations should be to ensure the health and well-being of young people. This does mean making sure that adults who work regularly with minors have been properly background-checked and have been given child abuse prevention training. Supportive adults should follow both church guidelines and good sense when it comes to connecting with teens both in-person and online. We want to ensure that every precaution is taken to protect the children and teens in our congregation's care.

If, as a leader in your congregation, you suspect that any adult is making a youth uncomfortable, do not hesitate to deal with the situation head-on. There have been far too many examples of adults in congregations taking advantage of the trust allowed in a congregational setting to grievously hurt young people. Should a youth ever tell you that an adult, even a key trusted leader in your congregation, has been inappropriate with them in any way, please take it very seriously and follow the protocols you have in place to ensure it is handled appropriately. If you don't have any protocols, please consider creating them immediately. The desire to have supportive adults and to give them the benefit of the doubt does not supersede our responsibility to report abuse of any kind.

We use the word *relationship* often when talking about supportive adults, but we want to be clear about what that relationship is. The youth who you care for in your congregation are not your friends or your peers. The relationship you form also doesn't replace the parental or guardian role. Supportive adults hold a unique place where they can cheer young people on, listen to them well, and mentor them. This relationship, however, like all important relationships, must come with clear boundaries. There should be parts of your life that you do not share with teens.

This doesn't mean you are inauthentic, but it does mean there are topics of conversation and areas of life where you do not tread. The teens in your congregation are not the primary place you reach out to for support. Conversely, teens cannot be misplacing their need for friendship on supportive adults. While supportive adults might provide "parental" wisdom and guidance at times, they are not the parent and should respect that vocational role.

With the proper measures in place, adults shouldn't feel as though they cannot approach teens to greet them and get to know them. Simply being aware and conscientious about how you approach young people is a good first step. Then, as you gain mutual trust and support, continue to set appropriate boundaries. It is easier to connect when you have a shared experience, either as a youth leader in programming or through other kinds of service. Often, those adults can help identify and engage other adults and the parents of teens as much as possible. We build that supportive net together. Just like any other relationship, slow and steady wins the race.

If you have adults in the congregation who want to engage youth, one encouragement is to have them start with a name and a question. They should learn a teen's name and use it in greeting him or her, then think of a question they might ask him or her. Encourage these adults to listen well to the answer and file it away. They could even add such answers and details they learn to their phone's note app if they are worried about forgetting. The next time they see the teen, have them follow up and ask a new question. They should continue this pattern until they find points of connection with that young person.

For example, ask a teen what he or she is looking forward to this week. If the response is that he or she has a basketball game, ask about the result of that game the next time you see the teen. And then add a question about what position he or she plays (especially if you understand basketball). Keep at it until you find out that you are both big fans of the same basketball movies or teams because the conversation develops and grows over time.

As you jump in and encourage other adults, you may find that adults feel too nervous or embarrassed to start that conversation. It is good to remind them that it is not easy to meet new people in any circumstance. Encourage them to simply be themselves as God made them. We should not let our own anxiety keep us from engaging with young people in our congregation. Teens aren't some scary predators; teens are people who want to be seen and known, just like you.

Finding and Engaging Supportive Adults

It is simple to gauge how many adults young people are connected to by simply asking who they would feel safe turning to if they had a question, doubt, or crisis. This doesn't mean they necessarily have or will reach out, but their comfort level in being honest about their thoughts and feelings is a good gauge of the relationship. Doing this regularly can help you give some practical goals in helping youth feel more connected.

One of the easiest ways to make the connection between teens and adults is during youth ministry programming. The regular interaction and shared time together are perfect for helping adults not only build relationships but teach and share the Gospel. Youth ministry leaders should take advantage of the programming time by making sure the adults they invite are thinking of themselves not just as chaperones or drivers but as relationship-builders. It is also a useful activity to have a list of all the teens in your congregation and go through them with your adult leaders. You may be surprised who adults know or don't know much about.

It can be a bit more difficult to connect youth with adults outside of youth ministry programming, but no less valuable. Faithful adults can come from about anywhere. In fact, many of the adults who champion or care for teens come from unexpected places. Adults can find themselves sitting next to families at a potluck and strike up a conversation. They can catch a teen wearing a hat or shirt with a sports logo that connects to a shared support for a team. Wherever the connection comes from, congregations that talk about the value of supportive adults widely may find them from all corners of the congregation.

As you look for supportive adults, keep an eye out for adults who show warmth, challenge, and grace. These adults are often ones who can be empathetic and assured when they spend time with teens. If you want your youth ministry to be one with an environment of warmth, challenge, and grace, it's important that those qualities are embodied in the supportive adults you engage.

As a youth leader, it can be hard to find volunteers to assist in programming. It may seem overwhelming to think about how to find more supportive adults. If you are finding that it is difficult to get youth and adults engaged, don't hesitate to create programs that put them together in ways that are comfortable for both. This can include meals together or chances to tell stories. It can be off-putting and uncomfortable to simply assign youth and adults to be a mentor relationship. But finding ways for adults to choose a prayer partner, or for a youth to ask an adult for help learning a service task at church, can be particularly powerful.

If you are not a pastor yourself, consider getting your pastor involved. Even if a pastor does not become a supportive adult to every teen, it is important for youth to feel a connection with him. While they might spend dedicated time with the pastor during confirmation class, it's important to continue that relationship into high school and beyond. Be sure to invite your pastor regularly to your events, especially when there are ways for him to connect. This will help keep him connected with your youth and build a rapport that will allow them to be comfortable approaching him when they need to.

Supportive Adults and Technology

Technology has allowed us to stay connected with one another despite distance and time. There are beautiful ways that technology, and especially social media, has allowed us to create networks of support and connect with people who are passionate about what we are, even at a distance. Technology can provide an opportunity for adults to meet youth exactly where they are. Technology allowed many adults in the church to stay connected with youth and their families during times in the pandemic when it wasn't safe to meet in person, for example. There are some fantastic tools that can allow adults to interact positively in the lives of teens and support them from a distance.

However, like all tools, technology has a dark side. Most teens report having been bullied online.[7] Teens feel they must put up a facade of perfection on social media. They experience the fear of missing out and constantly compare their lives to the posts of others. Smartphone usage sometimes keeps us—teens and adults—from spending time connecting even when we are in the same place together.

These issues spill out into the church. Adults and teens can work together to use technology safely and put it away when interacting with people face to face. In our technological culture, the time we have in person each week in the narthex or

---

7   Monica Anderson, "A Majority of Teens Have Experienced Some Form of Cyberbullying," Pew Research Center (website), September 27, 2018, https://www.pewresearch.org /internet/2018/09/27/a-majority-of-teens-have-experienced-some-form-of-cyberbullying/ (accessed August 14, 2020).

in Bible study can anchor young people to real relationships and keep them from being pushed out and isolated.

There are many things happening in our technologically driven age that isolate us like never before. God calls us in His Word to be a Body together with Christ Jesus as the Head. As youth seek to better understand who God is and what God has done from us in Jesus Christ, they may question and doubt. They may struggle in both obvious and not-so-obvious ways. Technology allows us to check in more regularly into their lives and show them they don't need a facade with us. Supportive adults can stand by to remind teens that because of our gift of faith in our Baptism, no one—including them—ever needs to walk alone.

Never Walk Alone

One of Julianna's favorite parts of the confirmation program in her first congregation was her mentors. Every year, her seventh-grade students would identify an older adult or couple, typically retirees, to be their mentor. This mentor would meet with them and their parents once a month for two years. Julianna would provide a basic discussion guide that covered the same topic as what she had been covering in class. Confirmands and mentors got to know each other and mutually share how God was teaching them and working through their lives.

This culminated in a great moment each Confirmation Sunday. When the worship was complete, in the space usually set for announcements, she would have each mentor introduce the youth to the congregation. Now, most of the youth had been a part of the congregation their whole lives, but that didn't change this chance for mentors to proudly shine the light on these young people they had come to love.

Those mentors showed such joy in telling the congregation a few important things about their mentees: their favorite Bible verse, what they loved to do, and what they had learned together. In that moment, they were able to share a brief glimpse of the kind of relationship God desires for us to have across generations in the church.

In Ephesians 4:1–7, Paul writes,

I therefore, a prisoner for the Lord, urge you to walk in a manner worthy of the calling to which you have been called, with all

humility and gentleness, with patience, bearing with one another in love, eager to maintain the unity of the Spirit in the bond of peace. There is one body and one Spirit—just as you were called to the one hope that belongs to your call—one Lord, one faith, one baptism, one God and Father of all, who is over all and through all and in all. But grace was given to each one of us according to the measure of Christ's gift.

Adults who care for young people in our communities and congregations should consider how the Holy Spirit can empower us to walk in a worthy manner. We can show humility, gentleness, patience, and love when it is most needed. We can remind young people of their Baptism, which calls us to the one hope, one Lord, and one faith we have together.

Becoming a supportive adult will take time. Keep checking in with your youth and seek out opportunities for conversation and hospitality. There will be times when you will be unsure of what to say or do. You may even struggle to be supportive of some teens. Yet many of us would not be here if there had not been adults in the church who, through the Holy Spirit, pointed us time and again to the cross. Young people want to know they are valued and loved by God, by their parents, and by other adults.

Engaging supportive adults doesn't have to be complicated for it to be effective. More than anything, it requires adults who are willing to make an investment in the lives of teens. As they invest consistently, they will find God can use them in powerful ways to care for young people and share the Word of God with them. The investment we work for here is a long-term payoff, not a quick return. But it is worth it as young people deepen their resilient identity as a baptized child of God.

> THE INVESTMENT WE WORK FOR HERE IS A LONG-TERM PAYOFF, NOT A QUICK RETURN. BUT IT IS WORTH IT AS YOUNG PEOPLE DEEPEN THEIR RESILIENT IDENTITY AS A BAPTIZED CHILD OF GOD

God will also bless you as you share experiences, help support their faith practices, and encourage teens to stay faithful to Christ. In the relationship, you will learn, grow, and be inspired by young people. They have much to teach and model as well. Youth are a gift, and we are constantly amazed by what a blessing they are to the church. As a supportive adult, I hope you are encouraged by how you see God working through young people.

1. Who were some of the supportive adults you had in your middle school and high school years? What impact did they have on your life?

2. How can supportive adults going through later-life phases engage and invest in the young people of your congregation? How can people in these unique situations impart wisdom to young people as they mature?

3. What are some of the stories in your life that might remind others of God's work and point to the Gospel?

4. Who is championing youth ministry in your congregation? How can you support and thank them?

5. How have you seen technology change relationships in youth ministry and in your life? How might you use it effectively to connect with young people?

SEVEN PRACTICES IN PRACTICE:
Supportive Adults

We talked with Christine Ekberg about how she finds, trains, and engages supportive adults in her congregation. Christine has served Our Savior Lutheran in Norfolk, Nebraska, as director of Christian education since 2008. She is passionate about working with youth and families of all ages. In her role as director of family life, she oversees high school youth ministry, family ministry, women's ministry, and confirmation. She is married to Brad and has three children. In her free time, she enjoys spending time with her family, playing volleyball, camping, exploring the Colorado mountains, and drinking coffee.

What kinds of supportive adults do you develop in your ministry?

Supportive adults can be youth mentors who work directly with the kids, those behind the scenes with office or food needs, or a worshiper at your church who might not interact with kids but support them with prayer and even financially. Not all supportive adults are in direct contact with youth. They can be worshipers in your congregation, youth mentors in your ministry, or both. A worshiper can pray for the youth. A worshiper can financially support the youth. A worshiper can help behind the scenes with youth by helping with prep items, office duties, or even providing food and baked goods. They might not have direct contact with youth, but they can still be a huge supporter of the ministry.

How have you engaged supportive adults in your youth ministry?

Encouragement and freedom! Let them lead in their unique gifts. Use current supportive adults to share their experiences with other adults. Build a team with your adults, not just the youth. As the leader, some of my closest friends are youth mentors I work with to engage with the youth in our congregation. Get to know them, get to know their gifts, and let them be equipped to build up the Body of Christ. I have built those friendships by working with them in youth ministry. We get to know one another personally and in ministry. This has created a team-like atmosphere. Youth ministry is about pointing youth to Christ, and that starts with the adults who have taken the responsibility to teach them. Build the adults up too.

What have you found helps supportive adults have long-term relationships with youth? What are some helpful boundaries to set in these relationships?

I have a whole packet on this! I will share the main points we touch on every year for supportive adults who are working directly with the youth:

Be present with the youth when you are here. *Be here.* We need to create a safe space physically and emotionally for our youth to build that relationship.

Youth want to know they are cared for and have a space of their own. *Friends* and *Cheers* are great TV examples of this. The song "Where Everybody Knows Your Name" says it all. Humans crave a space that feels comfortable and includes people who know us. Adolescents desire this even more than adults do. The church is a great place to create an environment that is welcoming physically, emotionally, and spiritually. It should be a space I can show up to where someone sees me and knows me—a space that's designed just for me. Physical space can be a youth room on-site or a space off-site like a coffee shop or someone's home. It should be a space where they know, "I am welcome here, even on my worst days."

We need to partner with parents. This includes communication about youth events and supporting them, even when their children complain about them (because what teenager doesn't?). We must remember parents are the primary role model, not us.

Make it personal. Be vulnerable, but have boundaries. Be open and yourself. Teens see through fakeness, or if you don't really want to get to know them. They appreciate when they can get to know you for who God created you to be. Being a supportive adult is not about you, though. It's about the youth and them growing in their faith. Ask them questions about themselves and point them to Christ through everything.

Move them out. Yes, this is the hardest one. Our goal isn't to keep them in high school ministry. It is to move them to the next stage of life, whether that's work, college, or the military.

How do you help engaged adults who aren't directly connected to youth ministry?

Share, share, share! Make youth ministry and youth known in your congregation. Share youth ministry events and highlights in the bulletin or newsletter. Share pictures from events, not just once a year after a trip but throughout the year. Have youth participate in worship and be greeters, readers, and musicians. Anything they are gifted in, let them do it next to other adults. When people see the youth active, they begin to see them as an important part of the church. We are all, every age, a part of the church.

How do you help adults connect with youth during celebrations, transitions, or crises?

Being present is one of the ways we prep for this. If we are present during normal times, we are already there when transitions, celebrations, and crises hit. Supportive adults as youth mentors aren't a once-a-year thing. It's a weekly interaction of caring for God's people, as Deuteronomy 6:4–9 says. This is written to *all of Israel*, not just parents. We are called as the church to point people of all ages to Christ, and those younger children and youth need some more helping hands to step up. We celebrate faith milestones, moments in a child's life where we see God working—Confirmation, Communion, driving and responsibility, and graduation. When we move them out, that doesn't mean the relationship ends. It should grow.

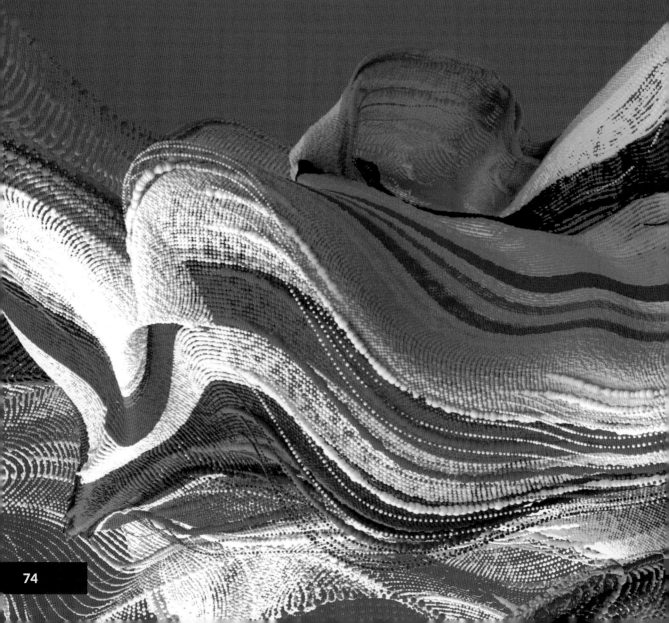

Chapter 5
ENGAGED PARENTS

Do not worry; you have not suddenly switched out a book on youth ministry with one about parenting. It might seem a little out of place for a book about congregational youth ministry to include parents as a crucial part of ministry. In some ways, we treat youth ministry and home life as separate realms with little overlap. Parents drop off and pick up from Bible studies and events with little information about what their children experience beyond what they can drag out of them in a conversation in the car. The reverse is true as well. In youth ministry, teens don't typically spend a lot of time talking about how their parents are helping encourage faith at home.

Healthy youth ministry extends past the congregation, into the home, and then back again. This is so important that engaged parents is one of our seven practices. Parents are gifted the role of primary instructors and examples for their children in the Christian faith. We see this in Scriptures like Deuteronomy 6:7–8, where God instructs households to teach the faith to children in the home and throughout each day. In 2 Timothy, Paul highlights the work of parents and grandparents by saying,

> **I am reminded of your sincere faith, a faith that dwelt first in your grandmother Lois and your mother Eunice and now, I am sure, dwells in you as well. . . . But as for you, continue in what you have learned and have firmly believed, knowing from whom you learned it and how from childhood you have been acquainted with the sacred writings, which are able to make you wise for salvation through faith in Christ Jesus. (2 Timothy 1:5; 3:14–15)**

While Scripture's clear call to parents is enough for us to include engaged parents in healthy youth ministry practices, we unsurprisingly see this in our research as well. We wanted to know how parents and guardians impacted the future of millennials' faith lives. In this research, we found several faith activities done in the home or as a family that correlated highly with millennials who continue to be active in the LCMS as adults:

1. Regular worship attendance by parents.

2. Frequent Bible reading at home. Praying with parents.

3. At least one parent having a service or leadership role in the church (both professional and lay).

4. Children have good relationships with both parents, and especially with dad.

5. Parents are comfortable with open discussions about life issues.

6. Parents are comfortable with open discussions about faith issues.

7. Parents are comfortable with open discussions about questions and doubt.

Each factor on its own contributes to retention. However, they are even stronger when they work together. More than two-thirds of today's active LCMS millennials claim that at least five or more of these characteristics accurately described their childhood home. Of those who left the LCMS for other church bodies or left the church altogether, only half claim to have experienced five or more of these characteristics growing up. This is not an exhaustive list by any means, but it gives us a starting point for how to practically define engaged parents.

What's great about what we found is that parents can help lead their children in the faith by doing *any* of these things. Parents may struggle to simply get their teenagers to worship throughout seasons of life. When this happens, parents can feel a deep sense of shame that they aren't doing more, and that shame can lead to increased isolation from the congregational community. Instead of leaving parents in their shame and isolation, youth leaders can help celebrate how parents are working hard to help their families receive God's good gifts. Youth leaders can help provide empathetic support through all stages of parenting, especially in particularly trying times.

When parents can make some intentional changes, we suggest they look at what factors they are already actively doing and then look to engage in one more. Once parents feel they have integrated that new practice into their family life, they can add another. There is no need to overwhelm parents and children by expecting them to do too much too quickly, thus making those changes unsustainable. What's wonderful is that we found every additional component parents added didn't just increase the impact but multiplied it.

The impact of engaged or disengaged parents can be felt all over youth ministry. Sometimes it is obvious, like when it's difficult to communicate with a parent. Sometimes there are more subtle clues to how engaged parents are in home discipleship, like how comfortable youth feel participating in prayer. While youth leaders have limited time with teens, parents have access to them daily. Even if youth are not overtly sharing it, their parents help shape their faith lives. In our Millennials and the LCMS study, nearly three in four millennials listed a parent as one of the most influential people in their faith lives. In every way, parents make a difference in the faith lives of their young people and subsequently on youth ministry.

Parents and guardians are critical, but they don't do it alone. Congregations can come beside parents, equipping them with tools and support in their vocation. When youth ministry is healthy, it partners well with parents, encouraging them and supporting them as they prioritize opportunities for faith development in the congregation, like participation in youth ministry. Coordinating families and congregations together in youth ministry isn't easy, but it is powerful in the faith lives of young people.

> PARENTS AND GUARDIANS ARE CRITICAL, BUT THEY DON'T DO IT ALONE. CONGREGATIONS CAN COME BESIDE PARENTS, EQUIPPING THEM WITH TOOLS AND SUPPORT IN THEIR VOCATION.

Engaged "Parents" Is Complex

This practice starts with a bit of a disclaimer. Using the right language to describe families is complex, and we struggled with the language when describing engaged parents. We know parents are the central teachers of their youth and model the Christian faith. Scripture says this. Our doctrine says this. Our research and the research of others says the same thing. To underplay the vocation of parents would be to lose their vital impact on the lives of young people.

Here is the rub. Not every young person has two faithful Christian parents. Some young people are being raised by single parents, stepparents, or extended family members. Some young people are in foster care, some are cared for in group homes, some are cared for by guardians, and some are in the process of adoption. The role of a parent can be filled in so many ways beyond two biological parents. In using the term *engaged parents*, we in no way want to minimize the important task many adults take on when they fill the role of parent.

Parenthood is a vocation God uses to nurture and develop young people, particularly young people's faith lives. God uses people who are willing to step into those roles, in addition to or outside of biological parents, in many different situations. We celebrate how God brings families together, even when the sin or brokenness of our world tries to tear them apart. God can use any family setting to share and encourage faith in Jesus. We don't want to limit God's work or diminish the incredible role a single parent, grandparent, family member, guardian, or other parental figure has in a child's life.

We also know that God can work faith in the life of a young person without his or her parents or even despite the efforts of his or her parents. In our study, some millennials said they came to faith without the support of their parents. In many of these cases, other adults stepped up to help ensure they had a supportive community. We do not want to limit the Holy Spirit's work in gifting faith exclusively to those whose parents were faithful believers.

So why did we include and use the term *engaged parents*?

Simply put, using the term *parents* helps us communicate. We struggled to find other terms or ways of speaking about this role that were more inclusive. However, we found that using other terms often muddled our understanding or intention in talking about parents. When we cite our research, we use the term *parent/guardian* in virtually all those questions, which can be difficult to say and read repeatedly. Using the term *parent* rather than *parent/guardian*, even if it isn't all-inclusive, eases communication.

By including parents in the seven practices, we also recognize that youth ministry isn't siloed or limited to just youth programming. Just as youth ministry is a part of the larger congregation ministry, all teens are a part of some family system. When youth ministries connect with teens, they also connect to and care for parents, siblings, and other family members. Even though not all families deal with the same issues and those issues can change over time, we didn't want to exclude this critical role.

The vocation of parent is so critical, and we hope that using the language of parent will lift up whoever is filling that role for a young person. When we say *parent*, we are talking about the person who is filling that role for a teen. Throughout this chapter and this book, we will take moments to remind you that those filling the role of parent are diverse. We want families and congregations to think of engaged parents in the broadest sense and to include diverse family structures in that role.

Engaged parents prioritize faith development by encouraging daily faith practices, especially during times of transition.

If you have looked at any family calendar lately, you likely did not find an excess of downtime. Families are busy meeting the many expectations of work, school, activities, sports, church, and more. Parents often feel like chauffeurs and administrative support. Today's busy families are constantly forced to make difficult decisions to prioritize their schedules and resources. Every commitment comes with its own demands. Expectations are set high for parents and teens.

Many things take priority in a family. How parents and teens prioritize what is most important in their lives and how they draw healthy boundaries can be a difficult and unique decision. As parents and teens struggle, they may often feel judged by other parents, coaches, extended family, and even the church. Youth leaders, especially church staff, can sometimes take an adversarial role against other activities. When youth leaders invest time and energy to help teens spend time with peers and in God's Word only to get blown off for soccer, choir, or homework, it can be hard for them not to take it personally.

Healthy youth ministry includes parents prioritizing faith development by encouraging daily faith practices. These faith practices include regular prayer, reading Scripture, confession and absolution, worship, and more. Many families pray together before meals or at bedtime consistently when their children are younger. The need to pray together doesn't change as children grow up. In fact, it becomes a chance not only to model prayer to a child but also to pray with and for one another. The same can be said of reading the Bible. Often, reading the Bible is relegated to personal devotion time, which is important. But spending time in God's Word as a family can be just as important.

The Barna Group, in partnership with Lutheran Hour Ministries, has studied spiritually vibrant households. While their scope and methods were different from LCMS Youth Ministry's research, both studies found similar qualities in families that were passing down the faith to their children and teens. Barna and Lutheran Hour Ministries characterized spiritually vibrant households as those that talk about faith together regularly, pray together, read Scripture together, and welcome non-family visitors into their homes at least several times a month. This combination of openness to conversation, spiritual practice, and hospitality were powerful indicators of spiritual health in the family.[8]

---

8   For more information, see The Barna Group, *Households of Faith: The Rituals and Relationships That Turn a Home into a Sacred Space* (Ventura, CA: The Barna Group, 2019).

These spiritual practices are not designed to be done out of obligation. They are instead done because the Christian life involves ongoing nurture in God's Word and love of our neighbors. These habits can be difficult or awkward to implement at first, but they will be developed over time and become easier as you do them. As children grow into teens and then young adults, it can be important for these spiritual practices to grow with them. For example, the way a small child interacts with worship on Sunday mornings should be different compared to how a teen or young adult does. While we want these practices to be consistent over time, we can adjust how they are implemented based on what is developmentally appropriate for each young person.

Encouraging daily faith practices is especially necessary during times of transition. Times of high emotion, stress, and adjustment can cause faith practices to drop in priority. There may even be transitions, such as a divorce or a job loss, where parents will feel nervousness or even shame when it comes to attending worship or giving an offering. Transitions, even the ones we anticipate, may be filled with ups and downs that can pull us away from those places and practices where God promises to empower our faith.

When parents point back to prayer, worship, and Scripture reading during times of transition, they help teach how important our faith is amid challenges. They remind young people that God is always with them. No family is going to do this perfectly. Not even the most engaged parent is going to model these practices with absolute consistency. There should be grace for when times throw off our plans and habits. Yet how we return to those models shows young people how to manage transition later in life.

As teens approach independence, parents can help them consider how faithful practice will continue during their next steps in life. Parents can look for churches or campus ministries during college visits. If teens are staying home for work or school after graduation, parents can help them consider how they might take on a new role at church and find new places for Bible study and support outside of youth ministry. By setting and managing expectations for spiritual practices beyond when they are at home, parents encourage youth to navigate the difficult time of life and faith as they become adults.

Engaged parents invest in the lives of their children by understanding their children's vocation and the culture around them.

Every teen is a unique creation and is continually learning to both embrace and hate all the things that make him or her so during adolescence. Perhaps you remember when you both loved what made you different and wished you could be like everyone else. It's in the push and pull of identity formation that parents can show up in powerful ways for their children. The way parents walk with their kids during adolescence pays powerful dividends.

Youth leaders often have the chance to talk with youth about vocation—how all baptized children of God are equipped to be God's hands and feet in the world. As youth leaders have these conversations, teens may be hesitant to identify the gifts and skills God has given them for their vocational roles. They may even struggle to identify who they can share the Gospel with. Parents and guardians are uniquely qualified to help young people discover their vocational roles and the gifts God has given them to share His love.

Engaged parents can step into these moments with insight that can't be found elsewhere. Parents observe their children when no one else can; they can spot skills and qualities that their children might not yet be able to identify. They understand who their children are and where they have the ability to love others in Jesus' name. Even in their most frustrating moments, parents can see their teens through the eyes of love. Parents and guardians know what their children are capable of, and they see the characteristics and abilities they bring to the Body of Christ. When engaged parents help teens see these things about themselves, teens are encouraged to form a positive, Christ-centered identity about who they are and what they are called to do. These vocational conversations also help teens see new and potential future ways to serve their neighbor through the power of the Holy Spirit.

We know that teens are surrounded by many voices. The culture can challenge their faith and lead them to questions and doubts. Parents need to be there to engage regularly in faith conversations, even difficult ones. The environment of warmth, challenge, and grace in your youth ministry can and should extend into the home. In our research, we found that today's active LCMS young adults are more likely than those who have left the LCMS to report having a good relationship with parents and being able to discuss questions of life and faith. Barna and Lutheran Hour Ministries found

> THE ENVIRONMENT OF WARMTH, CHALLENGE, AND GRACE IN YOUR YOUTH MINISTRY CAN AND SHOULD EXTEND INTO THE HOME.

that teens are more likely to talk with their mother, father, and grandparents than anyone else when it comes to questions about faith and the Bible.[9]

Parents and guardians can sometimes doubt that the conversations they have with their teens make an impact. In fact, parents may throw their hands up after an angry disagreement, convinced their teens will listen to anyone but them. Yet we saw in our research that parents and teens who had good relationships and were open to conversations about faith and life were more likely to be retained in the faith. Parents continuing to step into those difficult conversations with grace make a difference. Engaged parents are active listeners to their children around struggles, joy, interests, and gifts. At each stage of life, they can guide their children as God develops lifelong disciples.

Parents do not have to be experts in all aspects of teen culture. With countless social media apps, streaming services, online shopping, Twitch streams, and YouTube channels, that would be nearly impossible. Our culture today is always changing. We are no longer in a time where everything we watched or experienced on Thursday nights was shared by others who were watching the same shows as us. Our culture no longer sets up as role models the chosen few who have excelled as actors, athletes, or entrepreneurs. Instead, we follow influencers who are as unique in the content they create as they are in how they present it.

Parents shouldn't be experts in all aspects of teen culture, but they should be experts in their children. Social media is full of influencers. They range in age and types of content, but teens often follow many of them, listening to what they have to say about life, news, culture, and more. Parents should be able to list most of the influencers their teens look up to. This will range from youth to youth and shift over time. If parents know what kinds of messages their teens are hearing, they will be able to engage them in important conversations.

> IF PARENTS KNOW WHAT KINDS OF MESSAGES THEIR TEENS ARE HEARING, THEY WILL BE ABLE TO ENGAGE THEM IN IMPORTANT CONVERSATIONS.

While parents may not understand every social media app, they should be familiar with those most used by their children. Often, teachers, coaches, classmates, and friends will use social media to share information. Parents and guardians should know how young people are spending their time and who they are messaging. This should also include technology that might not be as obvious, like in the messaging function of many video games. Parents should think critically about what technology is appropriate at each age and be sure to monitor who teens are connecting with on their screens.

9   For more information, see The Barna Group, *Households of Faith.*

Engaged parents participate in worship, personal spiritual practices, and service.

In John 15:4–5, Jesus says, "Abide in Me, and I in you. As the branch cannot bear fruit by itself, unless it abides in the vine, neither can you, unless you abide in Me. I am the vine; you are the branches. Whoever abides in Me and I in him, he it is that bears much fruit, for apart from Me you can do nothing." If we believe parents have the primary role in modeling and teaching the faith to their children, they first have to be deeply engaged in their own faith lives. Parents who are connected to God's life-giving vine can bear fruit that young people can see. If we want our young people to abide in the vine and connect to Jesus, parents must do the same thing.

While many congregations separate adult and youth discipleship, the lives of faith within a family unit are intertwined. If we want young people to read Scripture, pray, attend worship, connect to youth ministry, serve, and lead, we first need to have adults, particularly parents, doing these things as well. Our research with millennials and the LCMS showed that active LCMS young adults likely saw and continue to see a high level of faith practiced by their parents. In fact, those least likely to see parents reflect faith claimed LCMS affiliation but no longer actively worshiped with a congregation. A parent's time spent receiving God's gifts overflows into his or her relationship with his or her teen.

FIGURE 6: IMPACT OF PARENTS' INVOLVEMENT WITH CHURCH AND FAITH PRACTICES

Of all the survey profiles, nominal LCMS Lutheran young adults were least likely to have had parents who were leaders in the church, read the Bible with their children, and attended worship regularly now or in the past.

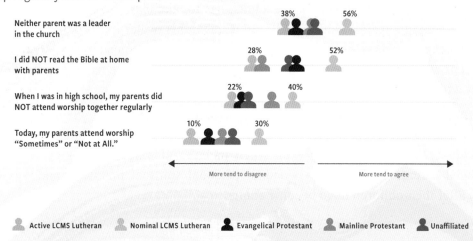

Source: 2017 LCMS Millenial Survey

Youth leaders reading this might begin to feel their blood pressure spike. Trying to practice healthy youth ministry for your teens is difficult enough. Now you have to worry about their parents too?! We are not trying to add more to your already full plate. Instead, we want to recognize that youth leaders should be supportive and cooperative with those in the congregation working to teach and lead parents. Youth leaders should look for opportunities to encourage parents in regular faith practices. It might not be the main priority for youth ministry, but supporting the faithful practices of parents supports youth as well.

When parents are engaged in worship and personal spiritual practices, it encourages them to reflect that to their children. When parents are filled up with God's gifts, they feel more equipped to prioritize and talk about faith at home. Conversely, when parents are disconnected, they may struggle to answer questions and doubts when these come up with teens. Congregations can work to make sure parents have the tools to read Scripture and pray on their own. Some congregations run Bible studies for parents parallel to confirmation or youth ministry. Others create packets or handouts that parents and youth can use together during Advent and Lent, when they are away from their home congregation, and during the summer.

Whether it be a parent, guardian, grandparent, or another family member, youth will tend to emulate the congregational involvement of adults in their lives. If that model isn't there, it is very difficult for youth to learn those priorities on their own. A teen who desires to be active in congregational and youth ministry might easily become highly engaged if his or her parents are already well connected in the congregational community, enthusiastically making sure their teen is present, and spending time with their teen at home talking about faith. Another teen with the same desire to be active but with little support from parents might encounter roadblocks as he or she struggles to connect with supportive adults, has to take extra measures to get rides, and has pressure against setting godly priorities in his or her life. As we encourage parents' engagement to encourage teen engagement, we also need to pay attention to the teens whose parents are not participating in the church. We need to provide those teens with additional support.

Young people don't stop looking to their parents as examples when they leave home. They want to know that time attending worship and connecting with a faith community is still important, even when parents no longer have kids at home. Engaged parents participate in worship, personal spiritual practices, and service, even after their children have become adults.

Supportive congregations provide parents with encouragement and support from other Christian adults.

Congregations have a role in encouraging and supporting all parents and guardians to actively engage in their children's faith lives. We have already talked about some of the ways congregations can walk alongside parents, but there are so many more.

One simple way to support parents is to help them understand what you are doing in youth ministry. This can be as simple as letting parents know what topics you are covering in Bible study. It could include inviting parents and families to a youth event so they can see what youth events entail. Help parents see the end goals of your youth ministry and get their input on what they believe their young people need. The more often you let parents know what is happening in youth ministry, the more they can connect it in other ways at home.

If parents are struggling to talk about and engage around faith at home, congregations can provide support. Some congregations offer specific classes that are designed to help teach or reteach important biblical principles for parents. Others provide small groups for parents with children around the same age for both study and support.

During the COVID-19 shutdown, we saw many congregations try to lean into and encourage parents to lead discussions and activities at home as an alternative to youth ministry programming. The results were often mixed and highlighted parents who felt empowered and equipped to step into that role and those who did not. It is important to remind parents that leading faith practices at home is difficult and that no family does it perfectly. Congregations can provide encouragement, practical resources, training, and classes to help parents become more comfortable sharing the faith at home.

Parents need people who can help encourage their faith practices, remind them of God's faithfulness, and give them good advice. This can come from older adults who are now empty nesting or come from other parents who are also raising teenagers. When other families can do life together, it not only helps develop additional supportive adults for teens, but it also gives parents supportive Christian friends.

Knowing how powerful the example can be, congregations can assist parents in attending worship, Bible study, and even creating opportunities to serve and lead. Midweek adult Bible studies are often scheduled when working parents might not be able to attend. Board meetings and other leadership opportunities may be out of reach for parents because of childcare pickup schedules or other schedule conflicts. Congregations should be conscientious in how they design their schedule to make it as accessible as possible for parents. Technology allows us to attend Bible studies and meetings via video chat software later in the evening. If a meeting can be done via email or at a time that runs alongside other programming, it can help parents engage and model positive congregational service and leadership to their teens.

What can congregations do when a young person doesn't have a household that is engaged and supporting their faith? This is where supportive adults and a faithful Christian community become absolutely necessary. God can work in all kinds of circumstances, including when a teen desires to know more about Jesus but comes from a home where parents are not yet believers. Youth leaders can identify and rally around these young people, making sure to engage several supportive adults in helping them. Youth may need assistance getting rides, approaching adults who are willing to get to know their parents in other settings, and getting to know supportive adults who can provide additional encouragement.

It is also important to remember that not every family is the same, nor does every family have two faithful Christian parents. When youth leaders design support for parents, they should keep in mind that these supports cannot be one size fits all. Fostering engaged parents can also mean supporting guardians, stepparents, extended family, and other adults who may have the same impact. Leaders can also be tempted to limit their scope to parents they know are strongly engaged. If we believe, however, that God can work in and through any person who takes on this critical role in a young person's life, we have to be prepared to support and engage families, no matter the form they take.

Team Effort to the Same Goal

A few years ago, LCMS Youth Ministry conducted a survey of youth leaders across the LCMS. While the sample population wasn't as random or as large as we would have liked, it did give us some interesting insight. We asked youth leaders, "What is one thing you wish your youth ministry had?" One of the most consistent responses centered around having parents who prioritize faith and partnered with youth ministry. It appears parents and youth leaders aren't always on the same page.

Barna's research found that parents and youth leaders did have differences in their expectations of youth ministry. Parents were less likely than senior pastors and youth workers to prioritize evangelism and outreach to teens as a part of youth ministry. Parents were more likely than youth leaders to put an emphasis on youth ministry being a safe space. Barna also found that parents had a high expectation that youth leaders were discipling teens and helping them navigate friend and family relationships. While that may be exactly what youth leaders are striving to do, that kind of discipleship and vocational teaching needs to happen well beyond youth ministry.[10]

Parents and youth leaders often have different expectations and desires of what youth ministry can be. Yet when parents and youth leaders are in sync, there can be a multiplied effect in caring for young people. In order for that to happen, there has to be strong communication, mutual trust, and a shared end goal. Everyone wants to see young people remain disciples for life. Through two-way conversation, this common goal can bind youth leaders and parents together as a team. They can support and have one another's backs rather than expecting one or the other to carry the load alone.

When it comes to setting schedules and priorities, youth leaders may have a deep desire for that young person and his or her family to prioritize their faith in Jesus first in everything. However, approaching parents and teens who are already struggling with and feeling guilty about the Law may just alienate them further. A youth leader's lecture on the First and Third Commandments might not have the hoped-for impact on parents and youth when looking at their calendars and how they spend their time. Instead, youth leaders and parents need to show challenge and grace. Spend time listening to each family's struggle and find ways for youth leaders and parents to support one another. If parents and youth leaders can't create a partnership, over time, animosity, bitterness, and negativity, all of which impact attendance, may grow.

That adversarial stance between youth leaders and parents doesn't help parents and doesn't foster a sense of partnership. Instead, if we want engaged parents, we must look for common goals and an open community. Youth leaders should work alongside parents to foster faith growth wherever they are. Parents may need empathy and encouragement when they struggle to raise teens. If parents feel they are at odds with youth leaders, then they certainly won't be honest about their

---

10 "Pastors and Parents Differ on Youth Ministry Goals," The Barna Group (website), Mach 22, 2017, https://www.barna.com/research /pastors-parents-differ-youth-ministry-goals/ (accessed March 13, 2023).

struggle or seek to partner with youth leaders to help teach the faith to teens. Parents and youth leaders have the same end goal and should find space to develop warmth, challenge, and grace as they work together.

INSTEAD OF TRYING TO MARKET, PROMOTE, AND PRODUCE YOUTH MINISTRY PROGRAMS AND ACTIVITIES IN A WAY THAT ATTRACTS KIDS TO DRAG THEIR PARENTS TO CHURCH, CHURCH LEADERS SHOULD START BY HELPING PARENTS UNDERSTAND THE "WHY" OF YOUTH MINISTRY.

One of the arguments we hear from different voices in the church is that if you make a children's or youth program attractive enough, flashy enough, or popular enough, then the parents will follow. If we could just get the best pizza and dessert, if we had games that were creative and energetic, and if we had teachers who always were compelling, the young people would attend in droves. The assumption is that if their youth want to be at church enough, parents will find a way to make that happen.

This argument has a couple of hiccups. First, the most important things we do in ministry are never going to be as popular or as flashy as the many offerings the world has. In a world that offers teens a multitude of flashy activities, entertainment at their fingertips, and so much more, it is nearly impossible for the church to compete. Even if it did, we run into the second problem: transportation. Until youth are licensed drivers with a car, parents are always going to have some veto power (unless teens can afford an Uber). So, instead of trying to market, promote, and produce youth ministry programs and activities in a way that attracts kids to drag their parents to church, church leaders should start by helping parents understand the "why" of youth ministry. Youth leaders want to produce an environment and programming that youth enjoy, but if you want consistent attendance, you have to make sure that parents are invested and understand the value of ministry first.

Parents as Youth Leaders

Some may be walking the fine line between parent and youth leader. This can be a particularly treacherous road, but it can also be tremendously rewarding. Parents serving as youth leaders need to make sure they are holding up both valuable vocations at the same time.

When a parent serves as a youth leader, he or she needs to set good boundaries and hold on to them well. The children of youth leaders can find they are called upon to answer questions, pray, or read more in front of the group. Mark is a pastor's kid and especially remembers being designated by other students to ask hard questions about the Sixth Commandment of the confirmation teacher, who happened to be his mother. Children of youth leaders may receive extra attention, which can both provide benefits other students don't have and can cause them to find themselves doubly in trouble. When parents work with their children in youth ministry, they need to remind themselves often to treat their kids just like they would any other young person.

One advantage to serving this dual role is that you often get a chance to get the insight you wouldn't already have. Have regular, honest conversations with your teen about how you are connecting in youth ministry. Perhaps your teen will be able to give you insight into relational dynamics you don't see or give you feedback on a game that didn't go over well. Asking for their input can help give them a chance to give meaningful feedback about youth ministry as well.

It also may be important for parents who are youth leaders to find other supportive adults who can connect with their children in youth ministry. Often, the children of youth leaders can feel as though they don't have the same support and outlet for conversation as other youth. Being sure these children are cared for, listened to, and supported by adults, just as you would for any other youth, can help them develop a stronger network of supporting adults.

Youth Ministry to the Whole Family

Helicopter parents. Over-scheduled parents. Health nut parents. Lawnmower parents. Forgetful parents. Free-range parents. Moms and dads receive lots of labels as they raise children. Yet many of those labels don't tell us about a parenting style as much as they bring judgment. If we know that social media has caused our teens to feel constantly compared to their peers, the same is true for parents. Every decision they make can feel like an opportunity for others around them to critique and criticize.

Just as every family is unique, every parent has his or her own approach to raising children. As youth leaders, we walk alongside parents of every kind. If parents are struggling and asking for help, congregations can provide support, reassurance, and resources. However, if parents aren't reaching out for help, it's not our role as youth leaders to critique parenting styles. Unless a teen is in danger, youth leaders may need to put away their judgment of parents and trust that God has given each parent a vocation to love their children and raise them to know Jesus as Lord. Even if we don't always understand or agree with the parenting styles we see in a family, as youth leaders, we engage and support both the youth and the parent.

Honor your father and your mother, that your days may be long in the land that the LORD your God is giving you. (Exodus 20:12)

When youth leaders teach the Fourth Commandment, generally, the focus is simply, "Honor your father and your mother." As we teach young people God's command to honor their parents, youth may point out all the faults their sinful parents have. Teens can see parents as out of touch or fun killers whose only function is to make them put away their screens, do their homework, and clean their rooms. As they try to establish their independence, teens may begin to push parental wisdom away in search of something else.

It's a powerful and important lesson for young people to think about how they honor their parents and authorities with their words and actions. As youth leaders teach this lesson, we don't want to leave out the key promise God includes with this commandment. There is a reason God gave us parents: so that our days may be long in the promises God has given us. While they might not see it now, teens need their parents. The wisdom, love, and support of parents helps shape young people as they develop into adults. Parents guide priority-setting and good decision-making and protect youth who are too often rushed into adulthood. Most importantly, God gave the gift of parents so that children may hold onto the loving salvation God has given them all their days.

If God calls us to honor our parents, as youth leaders, we should honor parents as well. While youth ministry may provide a valuable space several hours a week to spend time in God's Word together as believers, parents support faith many more hours a week, from the time teens get up to the time they go to bed. Healthy youth ministry needs engaged parents because youth need engaged parents.

DISCUSSION QUESTIONS

1. How engaged do you feel the parents of the teens in your youth ministry currently are in their child's faith life? in youth ministry?

2. Where might the parents of teens in your youth ministry be feeling overwhelmed or unsure and in need of additional support?

3. How does your congregation impress on parents the importance of their own faith life, worship, and leadership to their children?

4. How does your youth ministry train parents to understand their child's vocation?

5. How can your congregation find ways to connect parents with opportunities to learn and be connected with other parents for support?

SEVEN PRACTICES IN PRACTICE:
Engaged Parents

We talked with DCE Blake Brockman about how he partners his youth ministry with parents and supports their engagement in their teens' faith lives. Brockman is the director of youth and family ministries at Peace Lutheran Ministries in Antigo, Wisconsin. Blake is passionate about finding practical ways to walk with God, innovating in ministry, and mental health. He loves his wife, Hannah, sports, breakfast food, tacos, and being creative with writing and being creative on his YouTube channel.

How have you partnered with parents in your youth ministry?

Like many youth groups, we ask parents to be adult leaders and to attend weekly youth group and youth events. They come to meetings and help plan, evaluate, and execute events, fundraisers, and more.

However, we also partner with parents in more flexible ways. We invite and encourage parents to donate snacks, drinks, and meals for our weekly youth gatherings. We invite and encourage parents to help with large-scale fundraising events like an Easter breakfast. We have parents chaperone events from time to time—which is different from being an adult leader in our church with less responsibility.

We also invite parents to share their feedback on events and programming. For example, our church started a middle school youth group in 2017. Since then, we have gone from two events all year to one event a month, two events a month, and now weekly. Through that, we have changed times, days, and more after gathering feedback from parents. This has led our group to have forty-plus sixth through eighth graders weekly, which we have seen encourages parents to donate food, snacks, and drinks because they see the need. Hopefully it leads to parents wanting to help at events!

What are some of the reasons parents might disengage from youth ministry? How can we keep them engaged?

Parents are typically disengaged because they are busy. I have never talked with a parent about helping with youth ministry—or any ministry really—and been told, "I don't want to." The most common response I hear is, "I'm busy." They have kids in sports, 4-H, dance, band, some kids have jobs but can't drive, and so much more that requires parents to drive their kids around. Parents are also asked to volunteer for those groups, activities, etc. Parents are leading booster clubs, advisory councils, boards, and more. Oh, and most parents have jobs and personal lives of their own.

I'm becoming more convinced that the church needs to be flexible and approach this topic with a grace-filled posture. Yes, we 100 percent need adult leaders who can be there week in and week out, be the point person, and do all of those things. But what if you had a large pool of background-checked parents who pop in and out as their schedules permit? What if we included or created roles for parents that are more flexible, like ride-sharing, donating meals, and more? I believe we need to remember that a parent who reads the weekly text or email about youth group is engaged. Are they as engaged as John who is an adult leader and never misses youth group? No, but it isn't a competition, and I don't need everyone to be John. Overall, I think many churches and their leaders need to be ready to play the long game when it comes to getting parents engaged. The best way we can help parents stay engaged is to start small and be understanding of what is going on in their lives.

Parents often struggle with the many demands on their family's time. How do you help them navigate through that while encouraging them to prioritize worship and youth ministry?

The most helpful ways I've found to encourage parents to prioritize worship, youth ministry, and being active in the church is to be straight up with them and partner with them.

Think about the "traditional" confirmation experience for a second. Kids meet sometime in the week with their pastor or DCE. They sit in a classroom setting and listen to the pastor or DCE give a lesson. The lesson could even be interactive and super engaging. The kids receive homework, memory work, and more. But where is the parent in this scenario? Dropping off and picking up their kids, typically, without much thought about any homework that needs to be done. That's the opposite of what is on the cover of the catechism.

That model of ministry, which isn't just in confirmation but also in Sunday School and even youth ministry, creates a culture where parents do not need to prioritize being involved. Someone else is already doing it, and they have other things they can get done.

To help encourage parents to be more involved, we have changed not just confirmation ministry but also Sunday School to be more family-centered. Parents and confirmands do homework together, then the confirmands are taught by their teacher. Our Sunday School has parents stay with their kids the entire time. Parents and kids sing songs, study a lesson, and do a craft together. We've also been diving into the world of digital ministry to give parents quick and easy-to-use resources—like meal prayers and silly songs—that they can use at their pace.

Since we started actively partnering with parents, we have seen more engagement from them. However, changing that culture is hard. We've been at it for six years now. We have had to clearly articulate to parents why this is needed, how it benefits them now and long term, and what the expectations are. Many times,

the church is bad at communicating the expectations we have, let alone the ones God has, in a way that is clear and brings people to action. But being honest with them, sharing stats with them on the long-term benefits they and their children receive when they are engaged in the church, and clearly laying out the expectations is needed just as much as—or even more than—changing the format of programs.

How can congregations support parents and develop a supportive community for them?

Providing an avenue for parents to feel supported would be a great place to start. Personally, I am really fascinated with the idea of the church leading and hosting parent support groups. We need places where parents can come together, share what is going on—the good, bad, and tragic—and receive support and guidance from God's Word. Perhaps adding something like this to already existing and thriving programming would be a good first step.

I think what is important in all of this is to find out what works in your context—in your church and community. Ask parents how you can support them in mind, body, and spirit. Ask parents what they want to learn about. This will help you innovate ways to speak into the lives of your parents.

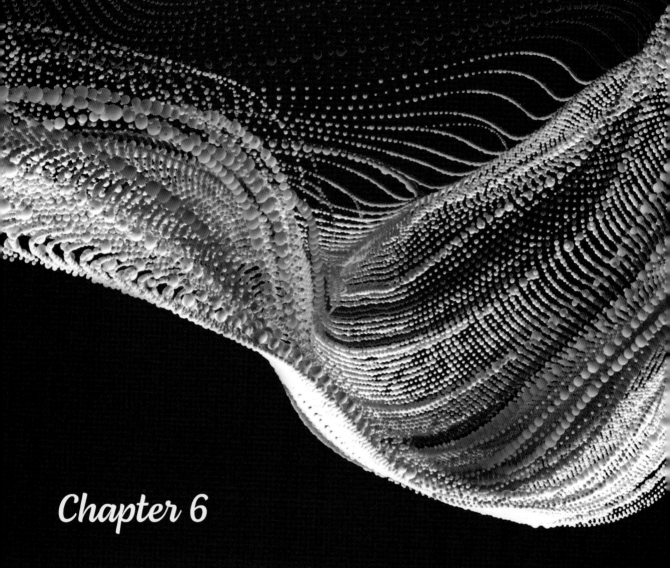

Chapter 6

OPPORTUNITIES TO SERVE AND LEAD

When we ask youth leaders what pivotal moments they experienced when they were teens involved in youth ministry, one of the most common answers is that they were given opportunities to serve and lead. Supportive adults and youth leaders let teens design youth programming, give announcements in church, assist with ministry to children, usher, decorate the church, and so much more. Looking back at their adolescent years, these adults can now identify the people who invested in them. They can perhaps see the risk youth leaders took to give them a chance to grow and how God used these moments to teach and form them.

Both Julianna and Mark could tell stories of how their home congregations gave them chances to serve and lead when they were youth. We were taken seriously by adults, given access to resources, and supported as we stepped into leadership roles. While we were not always successful in our leadership, adults offered us grace and continued to believe in us. In doing so, our congregations helped form us into Christ-centered servant leaders who sought to use our gifts to give glory to God and build the church.

Congregations, parents, and even teens sometimes forget youth become adult members of the congregation during the Rite of Confirmation. As our culture continues prolonging adolescence (the time from puberty to adulthood), Confirmation as a milestone into adulthood around fourteen years old can seem out of place. Teens are still growing and developing. They are still living with families. Yet Confirmation is a time when young people publicly proclaim their baptismal faith and step into the expectations of adult members, including service and leadership.

Healthy youth ministry recognizes the capability of teens and how God can work through them as servant leaders. Youth leaders can set high expectations for young people, engaging them regularly in opportunities to give input, serve, and lead. In living out their vocation as adult members of a congregation, post-Confirmation youth can feel a sense of ownership, build relationships, and positively impact their congregation and community.

Unlike all the other practices, opportunities to serve and lead involve a bit of a progression. Each part of this practice moves from least to most responsibility and opportunity. Along each step, you may be focusing on a smaller group of youth. We suggest that youth leaders see how they can move from one step to the next with their youth individually and as a group.

Congregations identify gifts and skills in youth that can be used in service, leadership, and vocation inside and outside the church.

Teens are not a monolithic entity; God has uniquely created each one. Yet we often talk about them as a group, particularly when we are talking about service opportunities. Older adults reach out to the youth leaders and ask if "some youth" are available to help weed the flowerbeds. The Vacation Bible School director needs "a group of teens" to be small-group leaders. Not to mention the vast array of service that "the youth group" is asked to do. These are all important and valuable service opportunities in congregations. No doubt, it is important for these tasks to get done and for youth to be involved.

The difficulty comes in when congregations think of youth simply as warm bodies that need a task rather than people with particular gifts, skills, passions, and experiences. Before youth leaders can place young people in service roles, they have to know about them. What are they naturally good at? What skills have they been learning and mastering? What are they passionate about? What experiences do they have that might help? When youth leaders know these things, they can place them in a position to use those gifts, skills, and abilities effectively for the glory of God.

Teens are busy today, and they are often involved in a number of extracurriculars, sports, work, and more all at the same time. Teens will always surprise you with their interests and abilities. Julianna talked with a youth she knows well after worship, only to have them share that they had a guitar recital that day. She had no idea this youth had even been taking lessons! The only way to find the right fit in service leadership is by getting to know young people.

As youth leaders help young people live out their vocations (something we will talk about more later in the book), we can identify places where they are already serving others in the community. In doing so, we can hear how God is using them as His hands and feet in places we may not have been aware of. We can also see the gifts and skills they are developing in a different light. We may miss out on highly capable young leaders by not taking the time to get to know them well. We may find that teens aren't going to mention the promotion to manager they got at work or that they were elected president of a student organization. In missing those teenage leaders who are already getting experience in other areas of vocation, we may inadvertently make them think the church doesn't want their gifts or skills. Knowing each youth personally allows individuals to be seen and allows youth leaders to take them seriously.

Identifying gifts and skills is a great place for parents and youth leaders to partner. Both parents and youth leaders are going to have unique insights into what service opportunities a young person might be interested in and what training or support they might require. Working together, teens and leaders can find the right service and leadership opportunities for youth either inside the church or in the community. Supportive adults and parents can help identify where the youth may excel and then direct the youth to the appropriate opportunities or even design new ones.

Congregations invest in youth by providing consistent opportunities for meaningful contributions.

Healthy youth ministry invests in a variety of ways for youth to make meaningful contributions to both youth ministry and their congregation. Meaningful contributions are opportunities to give input into important decisions and provide feedback on ministry experiences, goals, and direction. Perhaps you can think of "meaningful contributions" as a fancy term for listening well to youths' opinions and perspectives, then taking them into account when making decisions in the congregation. God designed the Body of Christ to include members of all ages. Young people often have fresh takes, creative ideas, or different ways of seeing what God is doing in a congregation's ministry.

> MEANINGFUL CONTRIBUTIONS ARE OPPORTUNITIES TO GIVE INPUT INTO IMPORTANT DECISIONS AND PROVIDE FEEDBACK ON MINISTRY EXPERIENCES, GOALS, AND DIRECTION.

All young people can give meaningful contributions if the youth leaders seek out opportunities to listen to them well. This can be as simple as doing a yearly survey of youth to help get a sense of what their needs are or allowing them to choose the next Bible study series from a list of choices. The more consistently you can get input and respond to it, the more likely teens will be to give you their honest opinions. There are going to be times when the contributions teens provide are outside of what is possible with your current resources. It can help in those moments to be honest about what limitations you see and ask them to continue to help you consider how to take their input while not running over budget or stretching leaders too thin.

It can be especially important for you to try and find ways to get meaningful contributions from youth who may be on the periphery of your youth ministry. Youth who are active in worship but not in youth ministry programming might have helpful insights you can consider when trying to better engage youth and bring them into youth ministry. In the same way, youth who have disconnected from the church will have thoughts and ideas that might help you understand how to reach them with the Gospel and encourage them to continue to be connected to ministry.

It is important to remember that meaningful contribution doesn't necessarily mean that you act upon everything your teens suggest. There will be times when even if you listen well to your youth, you will not be able to follow their opinions and suggestions. In those moments, it can be helpful to circle back and give the youth updates but affirm that you appreciated their honest sharing. It is important, however, not to simply ask for input and then never utilize it or continue the conversation. This is a quick way to shut youth down from sharing. If they feel you are only listening to them because you have to and not because you want to take their thoughts into account, the youth will quickly start to dismiss your opportunities to give meaningful contributions.

Beyond youth ministry, congregations can seek out youth and invite them to make meaningful contributions to the congregation at large. Even if they cannot yet be voting members, teens can be invited to voters meetings and invited to share their thoughts on the topics presented there. While this may seem like an event that many adults wouldn't want to participate in, Gen Z sometimes struggles to trust institutions and organizations. Voters meetings and other forums of information can provide transparency in issues around budget, leadership, and other resources that youth will appreciate.

The congregation's leaders should be able to connect with teens and listen to their ideas and perspectives. This is particularly true of youth who are involved in serving in the leader's particular area of ministry. In some congregations, families are assigned to a specific elder who makes sure to connect with them regularly. Those elders can make it a priority to connect with the teens in those families. If youth are approached genuinely and regularly, leaders will often find that teens have some wonderful insights and unique perspectives for how to improve ministry and share the Gospel.

Congregations engage and support youth in service inside the congregation, in the community, and beyond.

Youth ministry can sometimes be treated as synonymous with high energy game playing, late-night lock-ins, and too much pizza and energy drinks. While it might include those things, youth ministry is not just a set of self-serving activities and time to hang out with friends. As we trace back youth ministry to Walther League in the late 1800s, service has always been a key component of what youth ministry does, and that continues today. Serving the congregation and serving in the community engages teens and, with the help of the Holy Spirit, helps them practice living out their faith in new ways.

Service is when people use their skills and abilities to help the church or community. Young people today are more likely than previous generations to define who they are by their activities, work, academics, and hobbies. As a generation that is inclined to action, youth are watching the church. They want to see if Christians really live out what they say and if the love of Christ really overflows to neighbors. They value service as a way for God to use them to show mercy and point to the Gospel.

In the Millennials and the LCMS study, 94 percent of millennials, including those who had disconnected from the church, said it was important for a congregation to be involved in community service. In fact, some reported that the lack of engagement in service caused them to look for other congregations that would give them opportunities to serve. Engaging youth in service opportunities in your community, across the country, or even across the world can have profound effects on both young people and those they serve. While these opportunities should be done with great care and consideration, finding ways to consistently serve alongside those in your greater community can provide an important bridge to your congregation and the Gospel.

Service creates a shared experience that develops relationships. Perhaps you have experienced how a service project pulls people together, gives them a common goal, supports teamwork, and provides a place to start a conversation. Opportunities to serve can happen in places where youth are introduced to adults with whom they might not have otherwise connected. Service activities can present a reason to practice working together as Christians, providing a concrete picture of how the church should operate together.

Teens are connected across the globe on their phones and other smart devices and are more keenly aware at a young age of what is going on in the world than ever before. As they enter a time of intense transition to adulthood, they ask questions of faith about what they see. They want to know if the faith we teach in our comfortable, couch-filled youth room actually changes how we understand and interact with others every day. Perhaps more than millennials or Gen X, Gen Z teens want to see how their faith moves beyond the church walls and out into a broken and hurting world.

Service provides a way for young adults to connect that faith to the world around them. Service helps us understand Jesus came to a world filled with very real problems and did not shy away from issues of sin, death, and the devil. He came, lived, and died for all our sin and brokenness. Service takes us into the reality of the mess of a fallen world. It reminds us of our need for forgiveness. As we engage in service, we pray that the Holy Spirit will empower us to share Jesus' love and sacrifice with others.

> SERVICE IS A GREAT OPEN DOOR TO HELP YOUTH EXPLORE AND DISCUSS HOW WE ARE JESUS' HANDS AND FEET.

Service provides an opportunity to teach vocation. Service is a great open door to help youth explore and discuss how we are Jesus' hands and feet. In doing so, they can gain empathy and humility to help them take a new perspective on the world and grow in their understanding of how God can use them in little ways every day. Youth may struggle with how family, church, and work fit with their faith. Service is a wonderful way to open up that conversation and teach how our lives are expressions of our faith in Jesus.

Creating Thoughtful Service Opportunities

There are endless possibilities when it comes to service projects. Some are as quick as sharpening pencils in the sanctuary for ten minutes during confirmation class. Others involve weeks-long trips to foreign countries. One of the more challenging questions for youth leaders is how to choose service opportunities. As valuable as service opportunities are, they have to be provided in a thoughtful and deliberate way. There are four rules we suggest for finding appropriate service opportunities.

First, service should include appropriate instructions and support. Everyone can understand the fear of taking an important test and realizing you didn't study the right material. No one wants to go into a project without the information needed to be successful. This is especially true of young people who may be coming into the service opportunity with a lot less skill and experience than adults.

Youth may enjoy tackling the outdoor landscaping work of your congregations, but if they don't know flowers from weeds or the right way to use clippers, they could end up causing more damage than assistance. Many teens are equipped to work with small children and love to serve in this way. However, they may not have experience in classroom management, they may not know what activities or snacks are age appropriate, and they may not know how to watch multiple children at one time. Instruction and support for youth who are serving is vital to their success.

Before youth are engaged in service opportunities, the adults in charge should consider how they can set them up for success. This can include training or setting them up with mentors. As youth learn, adults should expect to give them regular feedback on what they are doing well and what they need to do differently. If possible, adults can model the service first, do that service together with the youth, then give observational feedback as the youth do it themselves. This provides them with plenty of time to learn and feel confident.

Second, service should not be what adult volunteers simply don't want to do. In the work of youth leaders, there are always undesirable tasks—things that drop to the bottom of the to-do lists for as long as possible before they have to be completed. We will not always love all the ways we are called to serve our congregation, family, and neighbors. However, imagine if those above you at your workplace consistently and only asked you to handle the tasks that no one else wanted to do. What if your family always left you with the most difficult and disgusting housework? You might become understandably frustrated. You might start to question how much other people valued you and if they were ignoring your unique gifts and skills. No one wants to be relegated to only performing the tasks no one else wants.

Every youth leader has had the experience of someone in the congregation coming up to them with a need around the congregation and asking, "Why can't the youth do this?" The problem here is that these service opportunities are often last minute, at inconvenient times, or are undesirable tasks for adults. These requests may be presented because no adults have stepped up to a task. Youth leaders need to be clear about what opportunities they will encourage youth to do. Sometimes this means there are difficult conversations that must take place with other leaders.

There are absolutely things that teens are more capable of doing than older adults. Youth have incredible energy, enthusiasm, and endurance that adults might lose as they get older. There is nothing wrong with asking youth to serve at tasks that might be more difficult for those who are older. In fact, it might be a great joy for them to take on tasks that their age and vitality make them uniquely qualified to do.

The key here is that tasks should be given to youth with a clear purpose and with intentionality, not just because it was the last option. Helping youth understand why certain service work is necessary, even if it is unpopular or difficult, can help engage them. It can also help to have adults who are willing to do the task with the youth's help, letting them know we are all in the same service together.

Third, service should always be an ask rather than an assumption. This perhaps applies most to youth who are already highly active and engaged in your youth ministry. Sometimes ministry requires a volunteer, and since the youth are around, it is assumed they can help. Over time, this can build animosity and actually deter youth from wanting to be at church. While it may be necessary to simply tell a youth to help in emergencies, you do not want that to be the norm. Instead, youth leaders should practice asking youth to be involved in service. It is even better if that ask can be personalized based on their gifts and skills.

Youth leaders may be in a situation where youth are being "volun-told" rather than acting as volunteers. When this happens, it is helpful for the adult leaders to advocate for youth to be asked to serve based on their skills. For example, if there is a need for childcare at an event and a teen is planning to be present, an adult at the event cannot assume the teen wants to serve in that way. Instead, some youth leaders choose to have a list of youth and their contact numbers handy so the adult asking can reach out himself or herself. When adults have to directly ask youth for help, the adult can direct the service opportunity to young people who may be a good fit.

Fourth, service should be something that works with and brings long-term benefits to those who are being served. In our desire to shine the light of Christ and to serve others, we often treat those we serve as objects rather than individuals created by God. Looking for service opportunities means doing our due diligence and seeking out opportunities that treat others with dignity and compassion. One of the ways we can do this well is by seeking out long-term partnerships rather than one-time opportunities. This allows us to build relationships, learn, and work alongside people in our community. It is also important to be reasonable about what work youth are capable of doing well. If your young people do not have the painting, repair, or relationship skills for a particular service, it is better to pass on the opportunity rather than do it poorly.

It is not always as glamorous to find the kinds of opportunities that require less specialized skills. When you do, youth might not view what they did as having as much of a dramatic impact, or they might not come away with stories of how they "helped" as they imagine they would have had with more visible and specialized service work. Yet, by recognizing how service impacts others, you can avoid increasing injury to communities already in need for your own benefit. There is certainly more to unpack here than we have time to discuss, but in all ways, youth leaders should seek to help and not harm when encouraging youth to serve.

Congregations empower young people to be load-bearing leaders by providing training, mentors, and space to learn.

As you look for meaningful contributions and provide service opportunities, you will be able to identify some youth who are ready for additional roles and responsibilities. Identifying these youth helps to engage them as load-bearing leaders in youth ministry or the wider congregation. We are going to use the term *load-bearing leadership* to help distinguish this kind of role.

There can be many different formal and informal leadership roles in a congregation. Load-bearing leadership uses skills and abilities in roles that include decision-making, responsibility, directing people, setting goals, and utilizing resources. Just like a load-bearing wall can't be taken away without serious detriment to the house, a load-bearing leader is critical to the ministry they are serving. This means that leadership roles for young people must naturally include a level of calculated risk as they learn and grow into the role with God's help.

We know young leaders have a strong impact on the retention in congregations. In our research, we found that congregations that had at least one leader under thirty-two years old were more likely to attract young adults, retain young adults through high school, and retain youth adults in the LCMS overall. These leaders were not exclusively staff. In fact, most of them were lay leaders. The positive effect of young leadership in retention is also seen in other research. Barna's research found that 69 percent of practicing Christians in Gen Z had gifts, abilities, or skills they wanted to develop,[11] and 97 percent of practicing Christians view developing their gifts as a way to grow closer to God.[12] In *Growing Young: Six Essential Strategies to Help Young People Discover and Love Your Church*, Fuller Youth Institute reports that growing, healthy churches can be characterized by empowering young people into leadership roles.[13]

Engaging young leaders is a very simple, practical thing every congregation can do to help enliven the congregation and improve retention.

There are many reasons why engaging young, load-bearing leaders has a positive impact on the congregation. When children and teens only ever see older

---

11 The Barna Group and Lutheran Hour Ministries, *Gifted for More* (Ventura, CA: The Barna Group, 2022), 48.

12 The Barna Group and Lutheran Hour Ministries, *Gifted for More*, 58.

13 For more information, see Kara Eckmann Powell, Jake Mulder, and Brad Griffin, *Growing Young: Six Essential Strategies to Help Young People Discover and Love Your Church* (Grand Rapids, MI: Baker Books, a division of Baker Publishing Group, 2016).

adults leading, it can be hard for them to imagine themselves in those roles. Young leaders can be an example to other young people, reminding them that they have a critical role in the church. Young leaders bring a level of energy and enthusiasm to ministry that older adults may have lost. Experience hasn't eroded young leaders' hopefulness or caused them to limit potential ministries. Their imagination is endless and exciting. They are able to advocate for programming and opportunities for other young people. Their perspective can shine new light and empathy on their peers so that the whole congregation can better share the Gospel.

Finding and Supporting the Right Leaders

In working with young leaders, you can think of your work as coaching young athletes. They need to develop skills, be encouraged, and be debriefed every step of the way. As a coach, you may need to spend time explaining the "why" of simple tasks to set them up for success and keep them motivated. When a young leader fails, he or she can receive forgiveness, grace, and new opportunities to try again.

> AS YOU IDENTIFY YOUNG PEOPLE WHO ARE READY FOR LEADERSHIP, YOU SHOULD START WITH THOSE WHO ARE CONSISTENT IN WORSHIP AND DESIRE TO SPEND TIME IN BIBLE STUDY, PRAYER, AND SHARING THE GOSPEL WITH OTHERS.

As you identify young people who are ready for leadership, you should start with those who are consistent in worship and desire to spend time in Bible study, prayer, and sharing the Gospel with others. Think of these as the fundamentals of any sport someone must master before they are able to move toward something more complex. Putting a young person into leadership with the hope that his or her position will inspire him or her to prioritize their faith can be problematic. Instead, look for those who are already strong in their understanding of their baptismal faith.

As you find young leaders who are ready to step up their leadership game, they will need a good coach and mentor. Young leaders should have one or two key adult leaders who are committed to walking with them, giving good direction, and setting them up for success. Choose these mentors carefully, making sure they, too, are deeply rooted in the faith. Ensure mentors have the time and the temperament to dedicate to the task.

As you match up young leaders with mentors, consider personality, interests, and connections. Having a good mentor can help provide critical learning and a balance of encouragement and challenge to a young leader. You have to know your players to be able to coach them well. Some young leaders are going to want a lot of feedback while others are going to want more freedom. Some young leaders need adults who can carefully rein them in while others are going to need someone who can push them out of their comfort zone. When these connections work well, both the younger and more experienced leader can benefit.

Part of developing a healthy environment for young leaders is to be sure to debrief, especially after a big event. This debrief doesn't have to be formal or time-consuming. Debriefing should allow you to affirm things that went well and to consider what things may need to be changed in the future. If emotions are high or things don't go as expected, there may not be a lot of conversation. It's okay to take some space to let it settle, but be sure to come back and discuss what happened later.

There is always room to grow, so focus on how young leaders are developing skills over time. How you approach this can teach them humility. This includes being honest about how you, as an experienced leader, may have failed to set them up for success. It can also help if you share past leadership experiences, both good and bad, with young leaders. They need to hear that experienced leaders have messed up a time or two before and lived to tell the tale.

Young leaders also need to see confession and absolution practiced by leadership when things go wrong. All leaders are going to make mistakes and damage relationships, intentionally or unintentionally. The church should be a place where leaders set a tone by trusting God's promises, confessing their sins, and receiving forgiveness. This is not a path young leaders will take unless it is modeled by more experienced leaders. Unlike competitive academic and professional settings, young leaders should find the church is a safe place to lead, fail, and find forgiveness and redemption.

Not every young person is a good fit for the leadership team. Frankly, not every adult is either. Choosing young leaders requires the same thoughtful consideration you would give to asking adults to step into leadership roles. Some teens are still developing their mental, emotional, and spiritual maturity and need time to grow before they are ready for leadership. Some young leaders are good fits but are already developing leadership in other areas of their vocations and don't have the time to commit. Other teens (and adults) do not want to lead. Selecting young leaders should be done with great care.

Adult leaders may naturally or quickly identify the most popular or charismatic young people as potential leaders. While their comfort level with being in front of people or their ability to engage peers can be an important quality, it is not the only one to look for. Be sure to also look for teens who are passionate about particular areas of ministry, like working with children, finances, and mercy work. You might find that someone who is quiet in Bible study is gifted in using technology or a very good teacher in small groups. It can sometimes surprise you whom God lifts up into leadership roles.

Fostering young leaders takes time and effort. In fact, bringing on young leaders might not make your ministry more effective right away. In coaching, new players always need time to acclimate, especially if they are playing at a more challenging level for the first time. For every positive impact a young leader makes, there will be time dedicated to teaching them and debriefing them. They will bring benefits to ministry that no one else can bring, and there will be times when you will see tremendous growth in both the young person and the ministry. Sometimes it will seem like raising up young leaders involves more work and resources with little payoff. Experienced leaders should not be discouraged when young leaders cannot be used as "plug and play" leaders like other adults.

Instead, consider engaging young leaders as a long-term investment in the church. The time, energy, and resources you invest now will pay dividends down the road. Sometimes the payoff is not even for your team but for the campus ministry or future congregations where these young people will land. Young leaders may only be with you for a short season. In fact, the number of transitions they experience might mean that they have to leave leadership for a time and then return. Some young adults in our research talked about not feeling welcome in leadership while they were youth because they were in a time of life when they could not commit to a term of a year or two on boards. While this might be frustrating for experienced leaders and difficult for the ministry, it is worth it in the long run to engage these leaders for as long as you can have them on your team.

Passing the Torch without Setting Everything Ablaze

Training new leaders and transitioning experienced leaders is difficult in work settings, families, communities, and congregations. It requires commitment, grace, and a willingness among all involved to walk together toward the same goals. When congregations are looking to pass the torch to young leadership, they may experience pitfalls along the way. Mentors and young leaders may stumble, but there are some ways to prevent setting everything ablaze.

Experienced leaders need to prepare themselves before engaging young leaders. If leadership transition is a priority and not lip service, then experienced leaders will proactively do the work to make transitions successful. Existing church leaders may struggle to put aside their own egos or agendas to empower new leaders. When leaders have committed to a youth ministry for years, they have put their heart, time, and energy into it. When young leaders step in and, perhaps carelessly, try to make changes or give input, it can sting for experienced leaders. Experienced leaders should prepare for things to change, be open to new ideas, and remember that all leaders may approach ministry differently.

If experienced leaders aren't prepared, young leaders can end up in poor-fitting, powerless, or token positions. Sometimes this happens unintentionally when experienced leaders get nervous and undercut young leaders. Experienced leaders may hand off and then take back responsibility. When experienced leaders anticipate failure rather than success, young leaders will quickly spot this and disconnect. It is a risk to give an inexperienced leader some responsibility that might cause some part of ministry to fail, but it's important to trust them anyway. Asking young leaders to take on leadership roles only to be decoration can cause them to avoid leadership roles in the future.

In the same way, young leaders have to be prepared for a learning curve in leadership and listen well. Young leaders need to be reminded to be patient with the processes they might feel are holding them back. Church structure, both written and unwritten, can be difficult to navigate. Established church culture can suck the enthusiasm out of the most seasoned leader. Helping experienced leaders see the value of having input from other leaders or waiting for good timing can help them see the bigger picture of youth ministry.

The torch of leadership is easier to pass when it reflects the diversity of ages in the congregation. Established leaders have experience, knowledge of systems, and a critical understanding of history. They have relationships and connections that allow them to move more of the congregation toward new programs and change, paving the way for success. Young leaders bring energy to your congregational leadership. They are going to bring challenging questions and new ideas. Together, both sets of leaders can help define success so that the church can share the Gospel in new ways. Bringing all ages and levels of experience to the leadership table gives everyone a chance to grow and helps the youth ministry utilize the best of everyone's viewpoint and gifts.

> BRINGING ALL AGES AND LEVELS OF EXPERIENCE TO THE LEADERSHIP TABLE GIVES EVERYONE A CHANCE TO GROW AND HELPS THE YOUTH MINISTRY UTILIZE THE BEST OF EVERYONE'S VIEWPOINT AND GIFTS.

One of the major benefits of bringing on young leaders is that they look at ministry opportunities with new eyes. They ask a lot of questions; they dream big, often without hesitation. The natural response to this may be to immediately consider all the limitations that might make big ideas or changes impossible. Instead, experienced leaders can take the time to explain the resources available and provide wise guidance to help direct the energy of young leaders. In the end, young leaders sometimes need to be given the chance to try, even if things don't end up the way everyone had hoped.

Young leaders need a chance to fail. We want to be clear that we are not promoting that young people should be allowed to function unchecked, deviate from the Gospel, or sin against one another. All these should be actively prevented. Giving youth a chance to fail provides them with responsibilities that they might not fulfill and gives them the freedom to take chances. Young people know that they are inexperienced and are going to fail. Failure is something that can't always be avoided. Instead, what's important is what happens after they fail. Unlike in other contexts in a young person's world, the congregation can be a place where failure is given grace and where we know God is always at work through His Word.

Julianna had one of these moments a few years back with her young leadership team. They were leading a YouthLead program alongside the National Lutheran Youth Workers Conference. In the midst of this busy time, the leadership team made up of five young adults was asked to give a short speech on stage in front of hundreds of lay and professional youth leaders. Julianna had not planned for this, so the last-minute request threw the team into overdrive. Initially, Julianna tried to give them an out, encouraging them not to commit to something they weren't prepared for. But the team was confident that what they would share would be helpful. As the leadership team planned what they would say, Julianna tried to jump in, only to be reminded that the young leaders had the situation under control. To say she was nervous for them was an understatement. In the end, they did such a fantastic job sharing the passion and Christ-centered heart of young leaders that adults asked for their responses to be written out and shared widely.

God designed the church to work best when leaders can build mutual trust and work toward shared goals. Working together can help congregations avoid being stagnant. Experienced leaders can remove roadblocks and have the backs of young leaders when criticism comes. Young leaders can learn from experienced leaders and take what they have learned to energize programs that teach the Gospel and shine a light in their community. Experienced leaders can set up young leaders for success and provide relational credits to try something new. Young leaders can gain skills that benefit the church now and in the future.

This Is My Church

Please do not underestimate your young people. For too long, the church has expected too little from teens who are capable of thoughtful decision-making, strong leadership, and deep empathy. They are adult members of the church today, not just the future. When we treat them as children rather than developing adults, we miss out on all they bring and are capable of doing. God is working in and through them as they learn and grow in Him. This generation of youth is funny, passionate, brave, and capable. God has gifted them mightily, and we do them a disservice when we limit them.

Teens want to have a voice in what happens in their congregation. Younger generations are less likely to show institutional affiliation. Rather, they are looking for a sense of authentic community and purpose to their service. We cannot assume that they will wait around for their turn to serve and lead until they are adults. They have just as much of a vested interest, perhaps even more so, as adults in seeing their church vibrant and healthy.

Opportunities to give meaningful input, serve, and lead can be stretching, formative experiences for youth. God can use the results of this formation to connect them to the church in a powerful way. This is an important part of creating an environment of challenge. Young people are capable, but they will also want to investigate first. Teens and young adults will likely ask a lot of questions when it comes to service and leadership. They want to serve and lead well and to understand the "why" and the "how" of ministry programs. Their fresh eyes and interest may help better meet the goals of sharing the Gospel, building Christian community, and learning in God's Word. As they succeed and fail along this path, they can be reminded that all is done because of Jesus' love for us and through the work of the Holy Spirit.

In providing opportunities to give meaningful contributions, serve, and lead, youth leaders are helping young people to see the congregation not just as *the* church but as *my* church. Youth are affirmed that they are a part of the Body of Christ through their Baptism and are valued members of their congregational community. They are able to see the impact they create in the lives of others. Engaging in service and leadership helps them explore the role of the Christian Church in their lives and the lives of others. When these things happen, youth become more and more likely to see church as something to prioritize in their life as they transition to new adult roles and locations. They will see that their church provides a sense of belonging through the Gospel, and they will never want to leave.

DISCUSSION QUESTIONS

1. Think of the youth you know well. What skills and gifts do they have that can be used for service and leadership?

2. How can teens have meaningful contributions to youth ministry? congregational ministry?

3. What service opportunities do you provide for the youth in your congregation? How can youth grow in these opportunities?

4. How might you put up good boundaries to make sure the service opportunities youth are given are healthy and sustainable?

5. What might prevent your congregation from engaging young leaders?

6. Which young people in your congregation might be ready for leadership? Who can mentor them along the way?

Chapter 7

CONGREGATIONS HELP ALL YOUNG PEOPLE . . .

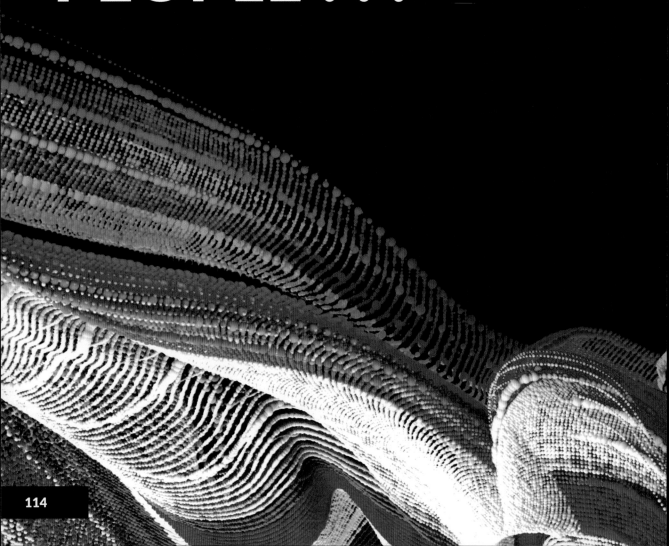

At a youth ministry conference recently, Julianna asked the question, "How do you want young people to be different because they were a part of youth ministry?" What followed was an uneasy silence. These youth leaders cared deeply for the teens in their congregation, so much so that they had traveled a great distance, paid money, and given time and energy to learn how to improve that care for young people. The moment of pause by these adults didn't reflect a lack of care for the young people of their congregation and community. It indicated how stretched thin many youth leaders are and how little time, direction, and freedom they feel they have to be more strategic in their youth ministries.

So, this prompts the question: How do you want young people to be different because they were a part of youth ministry?

You may be with the leaders in that conference room. Perhaps you have never given it much thought. Perhaps you have fallen into the pattern of offering youth ministry the way your congregation always has. Maybe the bylaws of the congregation dictate that there be a youth board that meets monthly and reports to the board of directors. Perhaps the same events fill your youth ministry calendar year after year, and leaders pull the same rotation of Bible studies from their shelves.

If that is the case, we know that God is working and active in His Word, prayer, and your time together. We trust that there will be fruit that comes from your youth ministry. We see those volunteers who are doing the best they can in the time they have to care for teens. Yet we also want to challenge youth leaders, parents, supportive adults, pastors, and other church workers to not neglect time to have a greater vision for what healthy youth ministry can be for you and the youth you lead. It takes additional work and conversation, but we do think having a view of the bigger picture helps you make decisions from week to week.

A Time of Change

If you love working with middle school and high school teens, you know it is a time of tumultuous change and discovery for them. Teens are messy, both literally and figuratively. All the teens in your congregation seem to be riding on waves of hormones, transitions, big feelings, and new understandings. One of the great things about working with teens is spotting growth. Sometimes that's a physical growth spurt that means last week's church outfit is looking a little short this week.

Sometimes it's the empathy you see them develop as they begin to really grasp the power of their words. Sometimes it's their spiritual growth as they begin to dig thoughtfully into Scripture and ask good questions.

In that time of change, youth ministry can provide a secure, loving place to ride those waves with adult leaders who have their best interests at heart. While sharing Jesus is simple, it's not always easy when youth seem to change overnight and are constantly experiencing new stages of development.

High school teens are beginning to learn at an abstract level with the ability to test a hypothesis and see multiple outcomes. They are learning to ask hard questions, build an argument, and form their own worldview apart from their parents. This can mean that while one youth may be ready to jump into more challenging aspects of faith during Bible study, another is overwhelmed to the point of checking out. It is a constant balance. Teens' brains and higher-level thinking are still forming and growing. You've probably seen a teen do something completely inappropriate one second, only to just as instantly realize the harm he or she has done. Healthy youth ministry steps into this development with the confidence that God's Word is alive and active, meeting youth where they are and answering their thoughtful questions.

At this stage of development, teens may be overly focused on themselves and how others see them. At the same time, they are growing into a more adult under-standing of what is going on in the greater world beyond their experiences. As they explore the wider world, they will grow in their understanding of brokenness in the world and test their ability to fix those problems. We see teens grow passionate about living out God's call to love others in His name, while others become dis-heartened and frustrated.

One of the major tasks of adolescence is identity formation. Teens are trying on new "identities" and assessing them to see what fits and what doesn't. The social and emotional process of developing identity and independence is not new. But in our culture, it can be even more challenging. The number of possible identities to investigate is exponentially bigger than it has been in the past and ranges far outside what is God-pleasing. This identity exploration is also happening online, where everyone can witness every step. Knowing how challenging this can be, youth ministry can be a place where identity formation centers around Christ, who has claimed us as His own in Baptism.

Some people will question your sanity when you tell them that you enjoy the chaos of youth ministry, but you aren't alone. There is so much joy in the difficulty and development. Healthy youth ministry embraces awkwardness mixed with growth in order to help young people cling tightly to their faith and share it with others in high school and as they approach adulthood.

Looking to the Future

We want youth ministry to be one of the ways God works through youth to produce an ongoing connection, trust, and dependence on Jesus. Time in youth ministry may end, but we pray the impacts are carried into adulthood. The closer a young person gets to adulthood, the more complicated life becomes. Vocational responsibilities begin to shift. Young people begin to make their own decisions on how to prioritize time and be stewards of God's gifts. Stress rises as youth face major decisions like college or career plans. As they make these decisions, look for opportunities to remind them of their Baptism and that Christ sustains them as they live out their faith in everyday life, regardless of where they go and what they do.

Youth may step into more serious relationships, prepare to leave their parents and siblings, shift from casual dating toward marriage, and think about starting a family. These changing relationships and life choices alter support structures, open new possibilities, and create new hopes and dreams. Youth ministry can prepare them for these new roles. Additionally, relationships developed in youth ministry provide opportunities to consistently focus on Jesus' love and forgiveness and how these bind believers together regardless of how other relationships change.

Youth ministry should always prepare young people for college, military service, or a career. With that transition, their relationship with their home church changes. If a young person remains close to home, many of their friends from church will likely not stay, and the support networks they need may falter. Many churches struggle to relate to an independent "young adult" out of high school differently than a "youth" who is under the authority of a parent and still in high school. If young people move away, we want youth to uproot and replant and flourish in a new context and perhaps a new city, state, or country. Each of these contexts has its own challenges. Helping young people transition takes love and investment. Your congregation may not see all the fruit born in this young person. Youth ministry can also bring heartbreak as youth leave for college, military service, or a career, and possibly even leave the church forever.

For parents, pastors, and youth workers, there isn't much time to provide youth the foundation they need to face their constantly changing world during high school. There is so much to accomplish in such a short time with a lot of distractions and demands. Healthy youth ministry takes a long view. The goal is for young people to be disciples of Jesus Christ as they transition into adulthood and for their entire lives. We hope every day of their lives is lived in the hope of Jesus and rests in His promises of love and salvation. What happens in youth ministry resonates well beyond high school. It is God's will and our earnest desire that the teens and their peers growing up in our congregations have faith in Jesus as their Savior now and into eternity.

Practices for Young People

The next three practices are our articulation of what we think teens aging out of youth ministry should have for their next phase of life. They are articulated differently than the first four because they are goals that are less about the ministry itself and more about what the ministry produces. Certainly, you might articulate them differently in your church or add to them. But our hope is that all youth leaders want young people to hold tightly to their saving faith in Jesus now and always.

Healthy congregations help all young people . . .

Deeply Understand Their Baptismal Faith

Develop a Resilient Identity in Christ

Live Out Their Unique Vocation

These practices come to life as God works through parents and other supportive adults like church members, teachers, pastors, and church workers. We see them lived out in an environment of warmth, challenge, and grace where there are opportunities to serve and lead. Christ strengthens youth to be lifelong learners who leave youth ministry able to independently nurture their faith in new contexts and lead by example.

Young people deeply understand their baptismal faith by listening to their Lord Jesus Christ. This practice focuses on Christian education and immersion in the Word of God as our source of truth, hope, and salvation. The work of the Holy

Spirit starts at Baptism as we are gathered into God's family. It continues over time as youth come to know Christ more through preaching, teaching, and corporate and personal study. Baptismal faith is nurtured in regular worship, prayer, formal teaching settings (like confirmation, catechesis, or scheduled Bible studies), and informal situations, relationships, and individual study.

Resiliency has recently become a buzzword in connection to our economy, mental health, and beliefs. Young people regularly encounter new experiences, ideas, and relationships that challenge their faith and understanding of life. It is not "if" but "when" youth face trials and tribulations in this world. In fact, some of the challenges they face will come specifically because of their faith. Resiliency is a quality that allows them to stand strong in their identity in Jesus. Resilient faith can recover when knocked around by sin, stress, adversity, and tragedy by returning to the foundation that is Christ and His Word.

Our Lutheran theology of vocation provides beautiful insight into life's purpose. It opens our eyes to the number of ways God uses us to serve others in the name of Jesus. The roles, responsibilities, and relationships in our vocations have been given by God—citizens of God's kingdom, citizens of our home country or community, family members, and so on. We want young people to see the beauty of God's design, His love for all creation, and how they are uniquely gifted to serve creation in His name. Vocation helps young people understand their gifts, skills, and passions in service to the Creator.

In our research, we saw God active where He promises to be. We saw the Word of God alive and active in the lives of young people and their families. We saw pastors and church workers proclaiming the Gospel and forgiveness of sins and teaching all that Christ tells us to obey. We saw God's love shown to youth, which allowed them to be known by their brothers and sisters in Christ. We saw youth show love to others, which made God's love for them tangible and personal. These final practices remind us of aspects of discipleship that are true for all ages and stages of life and accentuate aspects of adolescence, especially in the information age. If this book were to be refreshed ten, fifteen, or twenty years from now, these practices might have nuances or changes of focus based on the world in which young people and congregations would find themselves.

These outcomes provide opportunities to continue speaking to youth about how Jesus' love, forgiveness, and plan are for them. As teens grow in their individuality and independence, Jesus is with them. No one can believe for them; God works faith in all people. Engaging in these practices will help them transition into whatever lies ahead, knowing "Jesus is for you."

In designing the seven practices, we outlined what we believe young people need in every phase of life. How we teach them is going to change with age, interest, personality, and experiences. The seven practices are also going to be applied differently in every context. If you are using God's Word and Sacraments, there are any number of ways to make sure young people know who they are in their Baptism, that they are rooted in their identity in Christ, and that they are living out their unique vocations.

By articulating these practices as the end goal of youth ministry, we can effectively evaluate programming and resources. This framework gives us a lens to identify the needs of teens in our ministry. We can cast a vision for supportive adults, parents, and the wider congregation. While we know God is always at work in us and through our youth ministries, these foci help us put the most critical things first.

Many verses and accounts in Scripture helped us reflect on and finalize these practices. We leave you with two of Jesus' parables that provide mental images to consider. One is the rock on which the wise man builds (see Matthew 7:24–27; Luke 6:46–49). The storm came, the rain fell, and the wind howled, but the house didn't fall because of the foundation. The other image is the parable of the sower (see Matthew 13:1–9, 18–23; Mark 4:1–20; Luke 8:4–15), who spread his seeds with little care for efficiency. Much of the seed produced little or no fruit because of sin, Satan, and the ways of the world. But some of the seed fell on good soil and produced great fruit.

WE PRAY YOUR YOUTH WILL HEAR THE WORD OF JESUS, BELIEVE HIM, AND OBEY HIM.

What is our hope for how young people will be different because they were a part of your congregation's youth ministry? We pray your youth will hear the Word of Jesus, believe Him, and obey Him. We pray the Holy Spirit works in their hearts and minds to create fertile soil for the Word of God to produce faith, peace, and joy. We pray God will use you to provide young people spiritual nourishment and strength to fight against the evil one. We pray you will remove obstacles to understanding God's Word and will, and you will keep your focus on Jesus. We pray for God's wisdom, strength, and endurance to be people who point young people to the foundation that is Jesus and to rely on Him in all things. What a blessing to be selected by God to help build the foundation for young people and watch the Word of God accomplish much in their life!

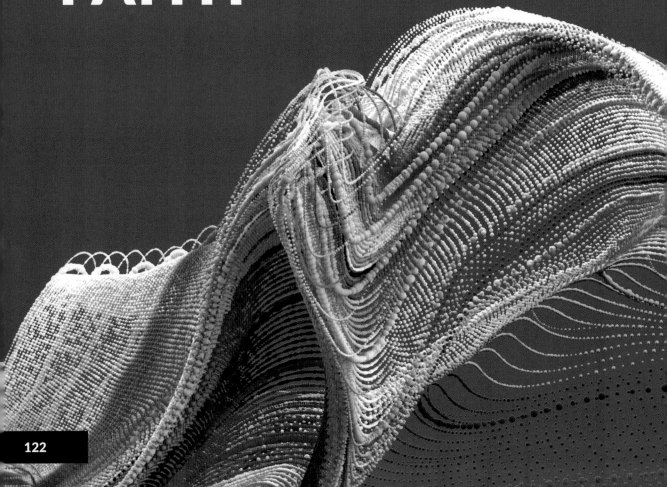

Chapter 8

DEEPLY UNDERSTAND THEIR BAPTISMAL FAITH

If you are working toward one goal in your youth ministry, this is probably it. New youth leaders will often start by focusing on this practice since most youth ministries already have a consistent time together for studying God's Word and prayer. Helping youth deeply understand their baptismal faith is a goal that Lutherans have historically worked toward. As a church body, we highly value understanding the faith God has granted us through His means of grace.

The practice of helping youth deeply understand their baptismal faith was one of the earliest and easiest practices we included. When we look at Scripture, it is clear. Jesus instructs His disciples after His resurrection, "And Jesus came and said to them, 'All authority in heaven and on earth has been given to Me. Go therefore and make disciples of all nations, baptizing them in the name of the Father and of the Son and of the Holy Spirit, teaching them to observe all that I have commanded you. And behold, I am with you always, to the end of the age'" (Matthew 28:18–20). Baptize and teach are commands that Jesus gives to the church. Healthy youth ministry focuses energy on the goal of young people who learn and lean into the faith into which they were baptized.

Healthy youth ministry helps teens deeply understand their baptismal faith. This sounds like an easy goal for youth ministry, but often it is more challenging than we expect.

One challenge is that while we believe everyone can read and understand Scripture, God's Word often prompts deep questions and reveals the mysteries of Christ. Youth leaders may feel ill-equipped to truly teach the depth of Scripture. Names are difficult to pronounce. Timelines can be confusing. Adults may fear that teens will ask questions they are simply unprepared to answer.

Still, as we teach God's Word, God promises us wisdom and the Holy Spirit. There will be times when we have to understand what is unclear in Scripture in light of what we know is clear. Youth leaders may need to do research and engage pastors and other church workers for help. If we want teens to grow into adults who deeply understand their baptismal faith, we have to be willing to jump into the depth and breadth of God's Word with them.

Another challenge may be our post-truth world. In 2016, the Oxford Dictionaries named post-truth as the word of the year.[14] In many ways, we can see the impact of a world that claims to be in a post-truth era. It seems that no one can agree on which experts or leaders to listen to for advice. What once seemed obvious in

---

14 "Word of the Year 2016," Oxford Languages (website), https://languages.oup.com/word-of-the
-year/2016/ (accessed May 17, 2023)

society is now up for debate. Our world is lacking trust in God, in institutions, and in our neighbors. Talking heads on both sides of the political spectrum often offer their opinions rather than the cold, hard facts. If there is no truth, what are we to deeply understand?

WHILE IT MAY SEEM WE ARE IN A POST-TRUTH WORLD, JESUS REMINDS US THAT GOD'S WORD IS TRUTH.

In John 17:15–17, Jesus prays before His crucifixion, "I do not ask that You take them out of the world, but that You keep them from the evil one. They are not of the world, just as I am not of the world. Sanctify them in the truth; Your word is truth." While it may seem we are in a post-truth world, Jesus reminds us that God's Word is truth. We can trust Scripture and seek to rely on it. Teens and adults alike should cling to what God tells us is true, even when the world around us seems to have no truth.

Yet another challenge comes up when Baptism feels disconnected from teens' lives today. This can be especially true for those who were baptized as infants. The event itself is outside of memory, only held in stories and pictures from their parents from what feels like a long time ago. Perhaps the anniversary of one's Baptism is a day not regularly recognized on the calendar, thus making its significance feel distant.

TEENS NEED TO BE REMINDED THAT IN THEIR BAPTISM, GOD DID NOT JUST ACT ONCE AND NEVER AGAIN. INSTEAD, OUR BAPTISM IS CONTINUOUS, AND WE CARRY IT EVERY DAY.

Whether teens remember it, the words of the Apostles' Creed were affirmed at their Baptism, and the devil was publicly renounced. Teens need to be reminded that in their Baptism, God did not just act once and never again. Instead, our Baptism is continuous, and we carry it every day. God was at work then and still gives good gifts today. Regardless of how long ago a teen's Baptism was, healthy youth ministry ensures that Baptism is continually called to mind and helps youth more deeply understand the faith given to them.

Working to understand our faith has challenges, but the result is vital. We see Jesus command the disciples to baptize and teach, but we know the disciples went into a world that would ultimately put them to death for what they believed. In the Reformation, Luther's life was threatened, but he stood firm in helping people read, know, and live out God's Word. Parents may struggle to engage and encourage their children with so much on their plates, but they are the primary teachers of faith. Youth leaders today can face the challenges of helping young people learn about the faith into which they were baptized.

The Importance of Christian Education

Helping young people deeply understand their baptismal faith is not just a goal of youth ministry. It is a goal of all Christian education and catechesis from the time of Baptism until the end of life. While we focus on youth ministry, we recognize that this is just a small part of congregational Christian education.

In some congregations, responsibility for educational programming is divided into separate boards or may have different supporting staff. Youth leaders should actively communicate their activities and goals with leaders focused on other age groups. At each level, a new depth of understanding can be added to biblical text. As children age, their ability to use the Bible independently grows, so the vocabulary youth leaders use to teach them can grow and develop as well. Sharing information about topics covered, languages learned, and even verses memorized can help prevent gaps and help future teachers build on new understanding.

Congregational Christian education often relies heavily on volunteer lay leaders who are willing and gifted to take on the task of teaching Sunday School, Vacation Bible School, confirmation, small groups, and adult Bible study. At each of these levels, the curriculum helps assist teachers and directs learning toward critical goals. Choosing a curriculum with specific goals and criteria in mind is helpful. A shared curriculum helps teachers teach similar topics at a developmentally appropriate level. When working together to choose a curriculum, teachers at different levels help create continuity from the youngest students to adults. There are different needs at each age and stage, and it is easier to meet those needs if everyone is teaching and engaging in the same direction.

Christian education programming is also a common place for youth to find service opportunities. Youth are often tapped as Sunday School helpers, Vacation Bible School leaders, and more. There are big benefits for teens who have passion and skill for working with young children. Nothing helps cement learning quite so well as having to teach the material. Teens who help teach and lead children's programs can gain both understanding and experience. However, we need to be careful that they do not miss out on developmentally appropriate lessons themselves because programs designed for them happen at the same time. Supportive

> HELPING YOUNG PEOPLE DEEPLY UNDERSTAND THEIR BAPTISMAL FAITH IS NOT JUST A GOAL OF YOUTH MINISTRY. IT IS A GOAL OF ALL CHRISTIAN EDUCATION AND CATECHESIS FROM THE TIME OF BAPTISM UNTIL THE END OF LIFE.

adults must guide teens away from missing out on material that will help them deeply understand their baptismal faith in the name of service.

It is important to recognize that youth ministry doesn't happen in a vacuum; it's part of a larger ministry of the congregation. Leaders of different age groups working together in the congregation can help everyone better care for children, youth, and adults. It may even spark opportunities for each level to create goals for each age group and for families that will help them choose lessons, activities, and programming. Christian education at every age repeats God's timeless truth over and over in new ways as we learn and grow throughout our lives.

Deeply understanding baptismal faith is the solid ground we build from childhood into the teen years and into adulthood. Congregational Christian education helps all to see that we never stop learning and exploring our baptismal faith. Our baptismal faith is so deep that we will never stop learning and exploring new things. The Christian education of young people is one part of a lifelong process of continuing to learn about and be thankful for the many gifts we receive in Baptism.

Youth live as forgiven sinners with the promise of eternal life through Jesus' death and resurrection.

If there is only one part of one practice that you include in your youth ministry, this should be it. This is at the center of everything. While we can give you lots of direction for healthy youth ministry, this is the one point that cannot be lost. Jesus is the heart and center of all youth ministry. Without Jesus at the center, there is nothing to distinguish what we do with teens from any other organization, program, or group. (Just because this is the heart of all we do in youth ministry doesn't mean you can close the book now!)

A healthy youth ministry centers around young people as forgiven sinners with the promise of eternal life through Jesus' death and resurrection. This promise is the deep foundation for youth to apply God's Word to the ever-increasingly complex baptized life. In these times of new learning, expanding freedom, struggle, and doubt, what can never be lost for youth is the ultimate importance of Jesus' death and resurrection. It provides them a place of confidence, resting in God's baptismal promises, which are theirs for a lifetime.

In the Gospel of John, God takes a moment to make sure we understand why the Bible is given to us. John 20:30–31 says, "Now Jesus did many other signs in the presence of the disciples, which are not written in this book; but these are written so that you may believe that Jesus is the Christ, the Son of God, and that by believing you may have life in His name." This is true for all we teach in youth ministry as well. Christian education will touch on numerous things Jesus taught us, but the one thing we want our youth to walk away with each week, each month, and into adulthood is that Jesus is our Savior, and through Him alone we have forgiveness and eternal life.

It can be easy for us to assume that the young people in our youth ministry hold fast to their faith in Jesus. Yet we can't leave that assumption unchecked. Adolescence is a time when many questions about faith arise, and teens may be hesitant to voice the places where doubt and disbelief start to creep in. Some youth may be going through the motions of faith practice because of familial expectation while not believing in Jesus at all. While the confession of faith in Jesus may be the simplest statement of faith we want our young people to have, we cannot assume every teen is holding on to that truth.

Similarly, young people are more likely to have friends who know little or nothing about Jesus. Thirty-four percent of Generation Z are religiously unaffiliated. That is a larger proportion than millennials (29 percent) or Gen X (25 percent).[15] Teens in your congregation will have many peers who were raised outside of any faith practice and may know

Generation Z was born from around 1997 to 2012. This generational group is defined as the first to be digital natives and to have no personalized memory of or before 9/11.[16]

Generation Alpha are those born from 2012 to 2024 or 2025 (at the time of this book's publishing in 2023, there was still no general consensus of the projected cutoff date for Generation Alpha). They are the youngest generation. While there is still much to learn about them, youth leaders should be prepared for them to begin to enter youth ministry in the next few years.

15 Daniel A. Cox, "Generation Z and the Future of Faith in America," The Survey Center on American Life (website), March 24, 2023, https://www.americansurveycenter.org/research/generation-z-future-of-faith/ (accessed March 13, 2023).

16 "Defining generations: Where Millennials end and Generation Z begins," Pew Research Center (website), https://www.pewresearch.org/short-reads/2019/01/17/where-millennials-end-and-generation-z-begins/ (accessed May 18, 2023)

nothing about Jesus or the basic tenets of Christianity. The deeper a young person's understanding of their faith, the better equipped he or she is to share it with others. If those religiously unaffiliated step into our ministry programming, we pray the Holy Spirit is at work as forgiveness and hope in Jesus is shared.

As Lutherans, the terms *sinner* and *saint* are often used to describe our sinful, broken, old self and our forgiven, justified, new self. We use these terms to describe the tension of our baptized life. Teens who deeply understand their baptismal faith can identify both their sin and how they are forgiven. While teens live in this world knowing they are both sinner and saint, in Baptism, saint is the name God gave us and the one that holds the most weight. We want teens to humbly recognize they are sinners and be confident saints and rest in God's promises for a lifetime.

Youth should recognize the work of the Holy Spirit, who brought them to faith, gathers them into God's family, and works through them.

CONFESSING THE WORK OF THE HOLY SPIRIT, "I CANNOT BY MY OWN REASON OR STRENGTH BELIEVE IN JESUS CHRIST, MY LORD, OR COME TO HIM" (SMALL CATECHISM, THIRD ARTICLE, PART 3), REFLECTS A HUMBLE UNDERSTANDING OF HOW WE ARE EMPOWERED TO CONFESS CHRIST.

Christian living is centered on receiving all good things from God. This includes our faith in Jesus. In response to the Gospel, we are motivated to obey God and show our love for Him. As young saints grow in confidence, they are tethered to the knowledge that the Holy Spirit is at work. The Holy Spirit works to transform the hearts, minds, and lives of young people. Confessing the work of the Holy Spirit, "I cannot by my own reason or strength believe in Jesus Christ, my Lord, or come to Him" (Small Catechism, Third Article, Part 3), reflects a humble understanding of how we are empowered to confess Christ.

Teenagers don't like to think of themselves as dependent. It is easier to think of newborn babies or those who are elderly as dependent rather than an energetic, sarcastic, seemingly indestructible teen. Adolescence is a time for gaining independence. During this time, youth learn social skills, make their own decisions, learn the importance of earning grades and income, and so much more. Pressures are all around them to study and play harder, practice more, and be more focused on the task at hand.

The call of John the Baptist, "He must increase, but I must decrease" (John 3:30), can be a far cry from what a teen is being told to "increase" in his or her life.

Teens are focused on increasing their skills, their social standing, or their follower count. In order for Christ to increase in their lives, they have to depend wholly on God's Holy Spirit. One tension of the Christian life is that the ability to bear fruit doesn't come as a result of our actions. It comes from dependence on God. A key part of growing in faith is listening to God in His Word and leaning on His wisdom, strength, and generosity.

Youth also grow in their understanding that they do not traverse the world alone. The Holy Spirit brings people into God's family, the church. God's family is a community made beautiful in Christ and different from the world. The Spirit works through agents like parents and pastors, as well as His means of grace, including water and the Word, to call and knit people together in Jesus. The church is where Christ's love for all people and the Spirit's transformational power is on display. John 1 teaches that God does not bring His family together by human will or through one's genealogy. Because of Christ's church, young people get the opportunity to appreciate their congregation as a cross-section of people they would otherwise have little interaction with in the world. God's people are brought together by the Gospel and given unity in Christ with Christians near and far. Within the community of the church, young people can also see the power of God on display as this unity propels believers to fight against Satan and the temptations of the world as they wait for Christ's return.

> GOD'S PEOPLE ARE BROUGHT TOGETHER BY THE GOSPEL AND GIVEN UNITY IN CHRIST WITH CHRISTIANS NEAR AND FAR.

Youth are encouraged to recognize how the Spirit works in their lives. This can be challenging. Youth leaders may need to help youth have eyes for how the Holy Spirit calls, gathers, enlightens, and sanctifies the church. When temptation comes, we can celebrate when the Holy Spirit works to help them resist. The Holy Spirit goes with them into a culture that makes it difficult to stand up for what they believe. We can encourage youth to see when the Holy Spirit empowers them to be confident, even when they are afraid to share their faith. The Gospel provides motivation for forgiven saints to live their lives according to our heavenly Father's will. The Spirit fuels youth to put their faith in action.

> YOUTH CAN SEE HOW THE TIMELESS TRUTHS OF GOD'S WORD, REPEATED OVER AND OVER, LEAD THEM TO A DEEPER UNDERSTANDING OF GOD'S LOVE FOR THEM.

The Spirit works in tangible ways when youth show the fruit of the Spirit. On their own, youth may fail to treat others the way God commands. But with the Holy Spirit, they can show grace and love. We can recognize when the Spirit helps youth prioritize their time and talents with God at the center and respond to stressors in a Christlike way. The Spirit is present when they ask good questions about how to navigate issues like sexuality, gender, and racism as baptized children of God. When youth leaders and parents see the practical evidence of the Spirit at work, we can celebrate and use this evidence as a chance to help youth more deeply understand their faith.

Allowing space for youth to recognize the growth of the Spirit can be an important learning opportunity. This may be done through reflection, journaling, devotions, and personal Bible study. Through this reflection, youth can see how the Holy Spirit gives confidence, patience, and endurance. They can see how the Holy Spirit has worked on their hearts to trust Jesus more in all facets of life and to care for all people. Youth can see how the timeless truths of God's Word, repeated over and over, lead them to a deeper understanding of God's love for them.

Youth regularly worship, study the living and active Word of God, pray together, and receive the Lord's Supper.

As young people grow, their appreciation for and desire to be engaged in spiritual practices should grow as well. Healthy youth ministry instills in youth the desire to be where God has promised to be—in His Word and Sacraments. By the time youth are preparing to leave home, youth leaders should feel confident that they will continue to seek these out by finding a new congregation wherever they land (a topic we will explore more in the next chapter). This goal certainly ties back to engaged parents and supportive adults who help them see the Holy Spirit's active work in worship, prayer, Scripture reading, and Communion.

One of the interesting findings in the 2022 LCMS Youth Poll was a distinct difference in beliefs between teens who attended worship regularly and those who did not. The poll showed that teens were less likely to understand and believe the basics of faith, like salvation being in Jesus alone, if they did not worship regularly. Youth were far less likely to pray on their own daily, read the Bible, or attend Bible study at least once a month if they did not attend worship regularly. While this was not a truly scientific sampling of LCMS youth, it does help show how receiving God's gifts during worship impacts the beliefs and faith lives of young people. While youth-specific ministry is beneficial, all young people should be encouraged to be in God's Word and Sacrament given in worship.

RECEIVING GOD'S GIFTS DURING WORSHIP IMPACTS THE BELIEFS AND FAITH LIVES OF YOUNG PEOPLE.

All young people should also be encouraged to be in

worship and receive Communion regularly. If youth leaders find that teens are attending paintball or the latest lock-in but not worship, that should be a cause for concern. Likewise, if teens are attending worship but aren't engaging in prayer and studying God's Word with their peers, that should be a concern as well. Pastors, congregational leaders, elders, other church workers, and youth leaders need to recognize they are all on the same team with the same goal: ensuring that youth and families are actively engaged in the practices that connect us with God and with faithful believers in our congregation.

Healthy youth ministry instills in youth the desire to understand and study God's living Word. Scripture is not just another source of information but the source of God's living Word, which God has given to us. Technology provides many with instant access to information, ads, and data from the moment they wake up until they go to sleep. Youth need a lens through which to process and understand all the information given to them. Amid all the voices and information, parents and supportive adults can train young people to listen to Jesus' voice above all the chatter.

Adults, especially teachers, pastors, and parents, are no longer gatekeepers of information. Instead of needing the expertise or instruction of an adult, youth can now quickly ask artificial intelligence or search for a video to help them understand a new concept or learn a new skill. With that transition, adults should help teens create filters or lenses to see all they encounter in a Christian way. We can't always be there to hold young peoples' hands as they scroll on their phones or do research online for school. Instead, we can teach them what questions to ask, how to assess the reliability of information, and give them space to bring us what they may struggle with. Deeply understanding our baptismal faith gives us the ability to take in media with a critical eye. Teens will grow to independently see when influencers, advertisements, and other media are attempting to pull them away from God's truth. The more confident they are in what they believe, the more confident they can be at dismissing the influx of pictures, posts, and platforms that tell them differently.

In our focus groups during the Millennials and the LCMS study, we heard many young adults who were active in the LCMS express frustration and struggle with the church. Some had been hurt by people in their congregations while others saw ways the church was failing teens and young adults. Yet they were faithful in worship, they received Communion, they attended Bible study, and they prayed. What became evident was that these young people deeply understand their baptismal faith and had developed a resilient identity in Christ. Even when it would have been easier to walk away, they said, like Peter in John 6:68, "Lord, to whom shall we go? You have the words of eternal life."

Baptismal faith is nurtured in regular worship, prayer, and formal teaching settings (like confirmation, catechesis, and scheduled Bible studies) as well as informal situations, relationships, and individual study. As we help young people deeply understand their baptismal faith, we can be confident that the Holy Spirit will be active in drawing them closer to the love of Jesus in worship, study, prayer, and Communion.

Youth are provided with deliberate age-specific opportunities to move toward key outcomes for young Lutheran Christians.

Every youth leader has had a moment where he or she made a cultural reference their youth absolutely did not get. In an attempt to make a hilarious joke and at the same time connect as cool, you quote that character and receive only silent crickets rather than raucous laughter. You might even double down by repeating yourself, only to see questioning faces and a distinct lack of eye contact.

Communicating with teens means understanding where they are and meeting them there. Youth have their own slang and cultural references. More than that, developmentally they are in a space between childhood and adult life. As we teach teens, we learn how to create deliberate age-specific learning opportunities for them that help them understand their faith.

In chapter 1, we discussed how we believe that healthy youth ministry is possible for every congregation. The pushback to this is often centered around how to have youth ministry when a congregation only has two or three teens who span across both middle school and high school. Hopefully by now you have seen how supportive adults and engaged parents can help create an environment of warmth, challenge, and grace while giving opportunities to serve and lead even in places where there are few youth or resources. It is possible, but this goal is more difficult with fewer youth.

We say difficult but not impossible. Age-specific educational opportunities are easiest when you have a group with kids who are the same age. With a smaller group, you often have to get creative. Some ministries utilize mentors while others create opportunities with other nearby youth ministries. In some cases, teens are prepared to join an adult Bible study, though it is helpful for them to have supportive adults who can discuss questions on their level. Youth ministry can also get creative in flipping a classroom that allows parents to do age-appropriate lessons at home with a time for connection and questions with supportive adults at another time. However it works in your context, helping youth study God's Word at their level is critical.

Deliberate age-specific opportunities can benefit from engaging with the developmentally appropriate space for teens we discussed in chapter 3. Creating this space helps youth open up as they learn and feel comfortable asking questions. Youth leaders can be reminded to take time to ensure what they are teaching challenges but doesn't overwhelm youth. Every youth ministry can seek to send its teens out equipped with vital practices, skills, and knowledge given through the Holy Spirit.

Confirmation

Youth ministry is often connected to the preparation for and Rite of Confirmation. Confirmation is a unique educational opportunity to help young people truly dig into understanding the faith into which they were baptized. Youth are challenged to memorize Scripture and the Small Catechism in a way that will hopefully stay with them in difficult moments. It models how to ask significant questions of faith, including "What does this mean?" and how to find answers in God's Word.

While not every young person and his or her family are engaged in the confirmation process, it is one of the few times pastors, church workers, and lay leaders can get intensive instruction time with (typically) middle school students. Families may return to regular worship or engage in confirmation programs even if they have not been active in prior years. This can be a key moment to reengage parents in the faith lives of their children as well. As much as possible, it is important to take advantage of that time, both in teaching and building relationships.

While the scope of confirmation is usually limited to learning and understanding Luther's Small Catechism, there is also space for other topics. In seventh and eighth grades, the time most common for junior confirmation, youth are learning to understand abstract concepts. This means some areas of theology are going to be more challenging than others. For many, confirmation can be a time when youth

> FOR MANY, CONFIRMATION CAN BE A TIME WHEN YOUTH BEGIN TO LEARN, PERHAPS JUST ENOUGH TO ASK GOOD QUESTIONS. WE PRAY THAT FROM THERE THEY CONTINUE TO ENGAGE IN DEEPER LEARNING.

begin to learn, perhaps just enough to ask good questions. We pray that from there they continue to engage in deeper learning.

Confirmation is not graduation. As young people are confirmed, their need for Christian education continues. As students enter high school, what we teach them can help answer key questions about who they are, who they are to others, and their place in the world. High school youth ministry and adult ministry can both build on things learned in confirmation. As we will fill out in more detail later, confirmation is only the start for resilient, lifelong learners.

Youth ministry should connect with confirmation ministry in some meaningful ways. While every congregation handles its confirmation a little bit differently, the more connections that can be made between youth ministry, wider congregational ministry, and confirmation the better. Active older youth might come into a confirmation class to discuss how what they learned has impacted their lives in high school. Youth leaders may join in lessons or even help teach so that they can build relationships. Youth ministry can help celebrate on Confirmation Sunday and encourage youth to join them in the future.

As we look to help young people deeply understand their baptismal faith, what time is more important than confirmation? While adults may not always remember their time in confirmation with great joy, it can still be a powerful moment in the lives of youth. In fact, in our Millennials and the LCMS study, we had one active LCMS young person say that Confirmation was a pivotal moment in his or her faith life because this person realized the gravity of the public profession of faith. It was in that moment of public proclamation that the Holy Spirit worked on him or her to see just how seriously he or she needed to take his or her faith. Youth leaders, pastors, church workers, and parents can work to take full advantage of this time of intense learning in the faith lives of young people.

How Will They Be Different: 40 End Goals of Youth Ministry

In youth ministry, a number of topics can be covered. That doesn't mean that devotional time and Bible study with youth should simply cover whatever Scripture or topic the youth leader found the night before the event (though we have all done that, and God works in that too!). If we keep the big picture of helping youth deeply understand their baptismal faith in mind, there can be a strategy and goals that help measure that growth.

The 40 End Goals are statements we pray teens know and personalize by the time they graduate high school. They aren't the whole of Scripture or Lutheran theology, but they are critical pieces of understanding baptismal faith. These 40 End Goals are designed to move youth from confirmation toward a deep understanding of their faith, which will guide them as lifelong disciples. We pray young people hear these key tenets in worship, Bible study, youth ministry, and their homes.

There are many ways to approach the 40 End Goals. Some youth leaders choose to deliberately focus on different areas for a specific amount of time, then move on to the next. Others move from area to area depending on the interest of their youth. We have even heard of parents who take forty days to discuss a statement each day. The 40 End Goals should not limit what youth learn in youth ministry, but they are helpful goals for youth leaders and parents to consider.

As you teach and have conversations around these 40 End Goals, be sure the discussions center around Scripture. Use *The Lutheran Study Bible*, the catechism, and trusted digital resources to help flesh out the conversation. Reach out to pastors and other church workers as needed. There is a good chance teens will have difficult questions or respond differently to a statement than you might expect. Treat those moments with warmth, challenge, and grace. Keep the conversation going rather than dominating or shutting it down with the "right" answer. Continue to engage and teach as long as it takes to help them more deeply understand what God says in His Word.

DISCUSSION QUESTIONS

1. How can you regularly remind teens of their baptismal faith?

2. Does your congregation have a comprehensive educational plan and goals for young people from Baptism to high school graduation? How does your youth ministry build on what is taught in Sunday School? Vacation Bible School? confirmation?

3. How does your youth ministry empower teens to be self-directed learners and help teens to bring faith into everyday life?

4. How do you help parents and other youth ministry leaders communicate God's truths to young people?

5. How does your congregation record a teen's worship attendance? How do you follow up with teens and their families who haven't been in worship?

40 End Goals[17]

Youth will be affirmed in their IDENTITY as a loved Child of God. Through the hearing and study of God's Word, youth will know . . .

My heavenly Father wonderfully created me. (Psalm 139:14)

I have fallen short of the perfection God desires and understand the temporal and eternal consequences of those sins. (Romans 5:12; 6:23)

Jesus Christ loves me and has redeemed me by His atoning sacrifice on the cross. This is the Good News, the Gospel of Jesus Christ. (John 3:16; 1 John 4:10)

Jesus calls me to faith and is with me daily as I live in baptismal grace. (Matthew 28:19–20; Galatians 3:27)

Christ feeds and sustains me with His gifts—Word and Sacrament—of which I am an active recipient for a lifetime.

In Christ, I am a new creation. (2 Corinthians 5:17)

In Christ, I am both a citizen of heaven and of earth. I trust Jesus that He alone gives me life to the full in the here and now. (John 3:16; 10:10; Philippians 3:20)

---

17 The 40 End Goals are adapted from LCMS Youth Ministry's "40 End Goals of Youth Ministry," May 11, 2020, http://www.youthesource.com/wp-content/uploads/2020/05/40-End-Goals-Resource-Study-Guide.pdf (accessed March 13, 2023).

I am simultaneously sinner and saint (a new creation), asking for repentance and resting in Christ's grace, forgiveness of sins, and promises. I am strengthened in my walk with Jesus through the work of the Holy Spirit. (Psalm 51)

I was not created for myself but for others. I am called to act justly and serve my neighbor, to love and show mercy, and to walk humbly with my God. (Micah 6:8)

God has redeemed and gifted me to care for those around me.

Youth will deepen their understanding of the critical importance of Christian COMMUNITY inside their families, individual church communities, and in the worldwide church. Through the hearing and study of God's Word, youth will know . . .

God desires to bless me with family, friends, and community. (Proverbs 6:20; Ephesians 6:1–3; Colossians 3:20)

Through my Baptism, God gathers me into His Body/community, the church. (John 1:12–13; Ephesians 4:4–6)

Christ gathers and strengthens my local church community and the Christian Church throughout the world through Word and Sacrament. With this community, I gladly hear God's Word preached and taught. (Luke 10:16; Act 2:42–47; 1 Corinthians 11:17–34; Hebrews 10:25)

Christ unites my church community in love, and we are strengthened to live in His love. (Colossians 3:12–17)

Christian communities, especially families, are places I can receive and practice forgiveness. (Matthew 6:12; Mark 11:25; 2 Corinthians 5:16–21; Colossians 3:13)

My Christian faith connects me to God's chosen people over time and space—the joys, challenges, sufferings, and celebrations. At the Lord's Supper, I join with angels, archangels, and all the company of heaven. Together, we worship and give praise to Jesus Christ, the Lamb who takes away the sin of the world. (Hebrews 12:1–2; Revelation 5)

The church embraces and values the diversity of ethnicity, language, and culture God has created in His community. (Galatians 3:28–29)

I do not have to face trials or questions alone, but I can ask Christ for humility to ask others for help and prayer. (Galatians 6:2)

Youth will better understand how to have HUMBLE CONFIDENCE in themselves and in God. Through the hearing and study of God's Word, youth will know . . .

By the power of the Holy Spirit, I confidently confess my Christian faith personally and in every area of my life.

Jesus Christ is "the way, and the truth, and the life" for life now and the life to come. (John 14:6)

Sanctification by the Holy Spirit is a lifelong process through Christ's Holy Word and Sacraments.

I can boldly go before God in prayer in my times of need, celebration, and joy. I pray about sinful temptations and ask for the Holy Spirit to protect me from them. (Psalm 17:6; 145:18; Matthew 6:8–14; Mark 11:24; John 17:15; Philippians 4:6; Colossians 4:2; 1 John 5:13–15)

Out of love for my neighbor, I strive to be a witness of Christ in word and deed. (Matthew 4:19; 5:16; Mark 12:31; Luke 10:25–37; Romans 1:16; 1 Peter 3:15)

This fallen world will bring struggles "against the rulers, against the authorities, against the cosmic powers over this present darkness, against the spiritual forces of evil in the heavenly places." (Ephesians 6:12)

When faced with troubles, I boldly trust in God's mercy and cling to His promises. (Psalm 5)

At times, it will seem the world or "culture" may have victory, but I will trust in the truth of God's Word and His desire for me. (John 1:9–13; Romans 12:2; Ephesians 6:12; 1 John 1:5–10)

This fallen world will bring tough topics and issues. God's Holy Word gives me answers and responses to these topics. I may at times struggle with these answers, but God's Word and promises are enough.

Every Christian will not have every answer. I may not always agree with other Christians. Using answers found in God's Word, I will listen with patience, engage in humble discourse, and engage with them (parents, pastors, church workers, other adults, peers, etc.).

Youth will grow in the understanding and living out of their VOCATION. Through the hearing and study of God's Word, youth will know . . .

God places me in multiple roles (vocations) in life where I share God's goodness and love (student, child, athlete, friend, employee, part of the Body of Christ, etc.).

Motivated by the love of God in Christ, I serve my neighbor to the best of my ability and put their interests first. (Mark 12:31–34; Philippians 2:1–4)

As a Christian, I love and respect all people and work as a steward of God's creation. (Genesis 1:28; Mark 16:15)

I rely on God to give me "daily bread" and strive to be a good steward of these gifts. (Matthew 6:11)

I show respect and honor to people in vocations who have authority over me and/or serve me (parents, teachers, police, pastors, church workers, etc.). (Ephesians 6:1–3; Colossians 3:20; 1 Timothy 2:1–2; Hebrews 13:17)

As a young person, I prepare for future vocations (citizen, employee/employer, spouse, parent, etc.) and strive to understand how I serve my world through these vocations.

I will prayerfully consider opportunities to serve the church in roles such as pastor, teacher, director of Christian education, deaconess, and other church work careers.

As a reflection of Christ's love, youth will learn and live out ACTS OF SERVICE AND MISSION to the world. Through the hearing and study of God's Word, youth will know . . .

I can support the mission of the church (locally and broadly) through the gifts of my time, talents, prayers, and financial support. (Acts 12:5; Philippians 1:4–5)

I can pray for the mission of God's people to serve their neighbor outside of their regular vocation (medical missionaries, servant events, mission trips, mercy work of the church, etc.).

I will prayerfully consider serving outside my regular vocations when opportunities provide themselves.

I trust the Holy Spirit to give me words to share my faith with others when opportunities become available. (Matthew 4:19; 5:16; Mark 12:31; Luke 10:25–37; Romans 1:16; 1 Peter 3:15)

Where God's Word clearly teaches, I will stand for justice and fair treatment in matters of life at all stages and help, serve, and protect the life and well-being of marginalized and vulnerable people.

Chapter 9

DEVELOP A RESILIENT IDENTITY IN CHRIST

Just weeks after Julianna started her internship in Florida, her community was hit by a hurricane. And then another. And then another hit, all within the span of three months. She prepared her home, figured out how to entertain herself by candlelight, and comforted her distraught family back in Kansas. Overall, she fared pretty well. But nothing prepared her for her first time back on the road heading to work after each storm. The sheer number of trees ripped down to the ground was stunning. It was as if a giant had come by and casually picked up trees and tossed them aside. If you have witnessed the destruction left by a hurricane or a tornado, you will know this experience.

What was even more interesting to Julianna was the trees that were still rooted. While to her the reasons why some were torn down and others remained standing seemed random, deep roots, protection by other trees, and design made for withstanding such winds meant some trees came out virtually untouched from the storms. Julianna discovered that palm trees fare so well because their long trunks are supple enough to bend without breaking or pulling up roots.

The imagery we often use when we talk about resilience is a tree. When a tree is deeply rooted, connected to water, and in good soil, it is very difficult to knock over. It can face winds, storms, squirrels, and more while maintaining its health and integrity. However, if the tree's root system is shallow or damaged, it can be much easier to uproot. Once that is done, it is incredibly difficult to stabilize and grow again.

We are deeply rooted in the identity given to us in our Baptism. As we talked about in the previous chapter, each Christian is both sinner and saint. God tells us who we are in Christ. As we understand more and more about our faith, our roots grow deeper in the rich source of God's Word. Deeply understanding our baptismal faith is vital, as is growing an identity in Christ that can withstand the pressures and storms of life.

Psalm 1:2–3 says of the righteous man, "But his delight is in the law of the LORD, and on His law he meditates day and night. He is like a tree planted by streams of water that yields its fruit in its season." When we spend time in God's Word, be it in worship, in prayer, or as the Spirit moves us to put it into action, we meditate on God's Law. We see our need for a Savior, repent, and receive forgiveness. But notice what that time in God's Law does. It plants deep roots so that it can bear good fruit.

We want young people to be like deeply rooted trees and have resiliency. Resiliency is the quality that allows individuals to bounce back and adapt when faced with stress, adversity, or tragedy. In some settings, *resiliency* means the toughness or durability of a substance. This word is used in many secular settings. Perhaps you have even used it in an educational or mental health setting. Perhaps you have used it to talk about the strength needed for a construction item or technology. In the seven practices, we will use it in a slightly different way.

Resilience is a characteristic that allows young people to meet new people, face new circumstances, ask for help when they need it, and engage in challenging situations while maintaining their identity in Christ. Healthy youth ministry helps youth know about faith and grow in trust in the One who gives knowledge, grace, and forgiveness. Resilient youth stand firm on the foundation that is Jesus Christ. This resiliency is tough and has the capacity to stick around even through the most difficult times.

In Scripture, we don't see the word *resilience*, but we do see similar words that describe what it: *faithfulness, perseverance, endurance*. Young people may know Bible verses, hymns, the Small Catechism, and every creed and prayer, but if they lack resiliency, they may be tossed about by the challenges of the world, the devil, and our sinful nature. Like in the parable of the sower, faith is like a seed. But when not placed in good soil, it will likely be scorched and wither.

In the Millennials and the LCMS study, we asked young adults who had grown up in the LCMS but who were now in another denomination or outside of the church altogether why they left. One thing that struck Mark and Julianna was how some were open about how they were taught what the church believed but not why. As a result, when they were faced with a more compelling argument, they changed what they believed. Certainly, this wasn't everyone's story, but it calls back to the trees that are well-rooted for resiliency and the ones that may not be. Fostering resiliency is about helping give youth the relationships and tools to be able to hear new ideas and be friends with those who believe differently without losing who they are in Christ.

In our divisive, sinful world, Christians are inevitably going to come across resistance. Teens will need their resiliency eventually; they cannot be hidden away in protected greenhouses forever. Youth ministry is a place of preparation for what teens face now and what they will face in the future. As they mature and develop a strong identity in Christ, they will need fewer supports.

If youth leaders are nervous about a teen's future, they should remember to put that worry in the hands of Jesus. It is God who provides good, deep soil and water.

God gives young people the ability to be humbly confident as they meet new people, discover new circumstances, or work through disagreements. Through transitions and crises, resilient young people will return to the means of grace as they face challenges in this world. We do not know what the future holds for those in youth ministry, but we pray with confidence, knowing that God has them in His hands.

Resilient youth identify with the life and mission of the Christian Church and seek to serve others.

A few years ago, a European bus company did a series of ads that featured groups of animals working together to defend themselves from predators. Their tagline was "It is smarter to travel in groups. Take the bus." These short videos have stuck with Julianna, perhaps because there is a grain of truth there. God did not design us to face this world alone; it is smarter to travel in groups. God made us to be an active part of the Christian Church, a group of believers who are brought into the mission of God to bless all people with life and peace.

Understanding the life and the mission of the Christian Church starts with understanding how God has been faithful to His people throughout Scripture. God created us to be in community and drew us together as His people right from the start. God gave Abraham His mission to bless all the families of the earth. God strengthened and protected Jacob, David, Jeremiah, and so many others throughout the Old and New Testaments. The book of Acts is a beautiful example of how God acted to draw misfits and sinners to His mission to proclaim the Gospel of Jesus. Our congregations are based on the same confessions as those throughout Scripture, and we are drawn together by the same God. We have the same mission they did to share the Good News of salvation through Jesus alone. Helping youth see the much wider history of the church, and even the history of your congregation, can help them appreciate how God has been faithful to His people and mission always, even despite our sin.

> GOD MADE US TO BE AN ACTIVE PART OF THE CHRISTIAN CHURCH, A GROUP OF BELIEVERS WHO ARE BROUGHT INTO THE MISSION OF GOD TO BLESS ALL PEOPLE WITH LIFE AND PEACE.

Resilient youth know they are part of a Christian community gathered by God. When we walk through life together, we are more able to navigate difficult spots where faith impacts or responds to real life. It is one thing to know what the church teaches about sexuality, but it is another to navigate how to be neighbors, classmates, and friends with those in the LGBTQ community. Teens may know what we teach about caring for our neighbor, but it is another thing to actively engage those struggling with monetary poverty. It is one thing to understand that we are connected, but it is another to lean into that connection to build resilience.

In our increasingly digital world, teens may feel disconnected from community and search for a place to belong. Youth ministry can be a breath of fresh air and a reminder to disconnect from technology and engage with one another. Seventy-nine percent of Gen Z report feeling alone either sometimes or always—the highest level of any generation.[18] Fifty-three percent of Gen Z said they wished they spent less time on social media.[19] The life and mission of the Christian Church is not flashy, easy-to-consume content. In fact, in the church, God calls us to service, not just observation. Everyone has a role. It is a real community centered in Christ and a place where disconnecting technology helps you reconnect to who God has made you to be.

IN FACT, IN THE CHURCH, GOD CALLS US TO SERVICE, NOT JUST OBSERVATION.

The reality is that for many of our young people, it may be hard to be Lutheran in their everyday lives. As culture shifts, it has become increasingly difficult to stand up for what you believe in. The church can be a place for them to ask for help and support when they need it. It is a great comfort and joy that youth do not go into these difficult spaces alone. Through the gift of faith, they are gathered into a community around the cross of Jesus.

Beyond their community, there are Christians around the world. The breadth of God's family is beautiful, and teens can take comfort in knowing the Body of Christ expands far beyond them. We may never worship with or even see our fellow believers across the globe, but we know they are also praying the Lord's Prayer, speaking the creeds, and reading God's Word. We are all one in Christ despite geographical boundaries, race, and socioeconomic situations.

Resilient youth remain humbly confident in their faith in the face of crisis.

As we considered how to describe a young person who has a resilient identity in Christ, we came to use the term *humble confidence*. Resilient young people

---

18 Cigna, *Loneliness and the Workplace*, 2020, https://www.cigna.com/static/www-cigna-com/docs /about-us/newsroom/studies-and-reports/combatting-loneliness/cigna-2020-loneliness-factsheet. pdf.

19 The Barna Group, *Gen Z*, vol. 2, (Ventura, CA: The Barna Group, 2021), 40.

stay well-rooted not because they are constantly on the attack or they passively let others knock them over. Humble confidence means they are aware of their sin and shortcomings and approach difficult situations as opportunities to both learn and share the Gospel. It also means that they have faith that God is good and will fulfill His promises to us.

Resilient youth can stand firm during unexpected crises. God's promises in Baptism provide a much-needed anchor when circumstances, thoughts, and feelings fail to bring comfort. Even in the most difficult of circumstances, God provides the faith to trust in His promises. Crises can look small to adults—like the loss of a game or a first breakup—but to teens, they can be world-shaking. Crises can also be issues adults may have to work to discover, like self-harm, sexual assault, or depression.

A crisis can be a serious threat, especially to a developing tree of faith. Depending on the intensity and type of crisis, parents, youth leaders, pastors, and other church workers will need to provide support. Think of this as staking a tree in times of heavy winds or covering a tree during freezing weather. Teens are still developing and do not always have the life experience or emotional regulation to weather storms alone. They need adults who are willing to share how God has provided and fulfilled His promises. They need adults who can remind them that this moment is terrible but temporary. They need adults to tell them who they are, even when everything around them or even within them says something different.

It is important for supportive adults and parents to prepare for moments of crisis and ensure their own posture or judgment pulls young people toward, not pushes them away from, faith. Adults should be sure to listen well and ask open-ended questions rather than jump to solutions. Dealing with a crisis is not going to be solved in one conversation, so engaging in ongoing support is important. Part of that support may be helping youth and families find professional help so they can process the situation and find rooted ground once again.

If the crisis includes the whole family, a parent or sibling's rootedness may be tested as well. It is okay to show struggle and emotions to your teen. Let them know you are with them in the struggle. But it may also mean reaching out to supportive adults who are outside the crisis and more equipped to help provide a listening ear and support. Likewise, there are times when what a teen is experiencing exposes pain or trauma in the adults around them. If parents or supportive adults encounter this, it is okay to work with the teen to call in other supports to assist. We cannot always support young people when we ourselves are shaken.

Some of the crises teens will experience will center around physical health or illness. They begin to understand the realities of sickness and death differently than children. Losing a loved one can bring questions about faith and God's promise to hear our prayers. While these types of crises are easier for youth leaders to spot, teens may also endure ambiguous loss. This can happen when important relationships end, when experiences that are highly anticipated don't happen as expected, or when they undergo different kinds of failure. Having eyes for this kind of crisis can help youth feel like they are seen and known by both God and adults who care for them.

Some crises occur as a consequence of teens falling into temptation. Teens are faced with pornography, the pressure from peers to drink alcohol or do drugs, or even the temptation to idolize fleeting things over God. Often these are held in secret or seem for a time to be manageable. Yet the truth is revealed in time, and when it is, teens often find themselves in a difficult spot. In these critical moments, supportive adults and parents can help reroot a young person into who they are in Christ. It can be helpful for youth to engage a pastor for confession and absolution. The Holy Spirit can work to orient teens away from temptation, strengthening them and helping them turn away from sin toward God.

Over the last few years, there has been a rising mental health crisis for young people. In 2021, the Centers for Disease Control and Prevention reported that 29 percent of high school students experienced poor mental health during the last thirty days. Some 42 percent experienced persistent sadness or hopelessness, with nearly 60 percent of female students reporting they felt this way.[20] More than 20 percent of high school students reported serious thoughts about suicide. About 9 percent reported a suicide attempt.[21] While these might be startling statistics, they are important to consider when helping young people navigate a crisis. Rather than approaching with judgment or minimization, youth ministries can have resources, and youth leaders can be prepared for when a young person struggles with mental health. Teens today are more likely to talk about their mental health struggles openly than they were in the past, but there is still an intense stigma around mental

---

20 "Youth Risk Behavior Survey Data Summary and Trends Report: 2011–2021," Centers for Disease Control and Prevention (website), 2023, https://npin.cdc.gov/publication/youth-risk-behavior-survey-data-summary-trends-report-2011%E2%80%932021 (accessed March 13, 2023).

21 "What You Need to Know About Youth Suicide," National Alliance on Mental Illness (website), https://www.nami.org/Your-Journey/Kids-Teens-and-Young-Adults/What-You-Need-to-Know-About-Youth-Suicide (accessed March 13, 2023).

health. Church can be a place where youth find ongoing support and strategies to help navigate and maintain mental health.

Resilient youth take on a posture of humble confidence as the world, the devil, and their own sinful nature try to unroot their faith. They recognize that Satan is a formidable adversary, they know the ways of the world are dangerous, and they don't take sin lightly. They understand the evil of their own heart and how quickly they can put themselves above others. However, in that recognition, the Holy Spirit points them to the One who has overcome it all and strengthens them in their stance.

> CHURCH CAN BE A PLACE WHERE YOUTH FIND ONGOING SUPPORT AND STRATEGIES TO HELP NAVIGATE AND MAINTAIN MENTAL HEALTH.

Resilient youth remain humbly confident in their faith in the face of transition.

Everyone faces transitions. Change is inevitable. Any gardener will tell you that there will be times when plants need to be repotted or moved. This can be difficult, however, to do well. Repotting or moving a plant can damage the integrity of the plant's roots. This kind of shift can only be handled well with the health of the plant in mind. Healthy youth ministries help youth prepare for their transitions in a way that helps their rootedness in Christ hold firm.

Some transitions can generally be expected, like graduation or entering the workforce. Others are less expected, like a parent's job switch or a move. These times of transition can be tenuous. Youth are at risk and exposed as they are disconnected from their usual support systems, including their home congregation. Youth may be faced with new, wonderful opportunities that seem to demand priority over their faith. Without proper preparation, it can be easy for transitions to be spaces where an uprooting means a loss of faith.

In the Millennials and the LCMS study, we found that only 54 percent of those still active in the LCMS in young adulthood said their church ministered to them during life transitions. That number was the highest reported of any group. Transitions are a part of youth ministry that are hard to program since they are often unique to each youth. Rather than letting youth navigate transitions on their own, healthy youth ministry engages relationships, instead of programming, to help them navigate their transplant. This can include providing moving help, setting up families to send care packages to college students, or taking youth out for coffee as their parents work through a divorce.

FIGURE 7: WORSHIP ATTENDANCE OF ACTIVE AND INACTIVE YOUNG ADULTS AT VARIOUS LIFE STAGES

Young adults who are no longer active went through a large drop in worship attendance in the years immediately after their high school graduation.

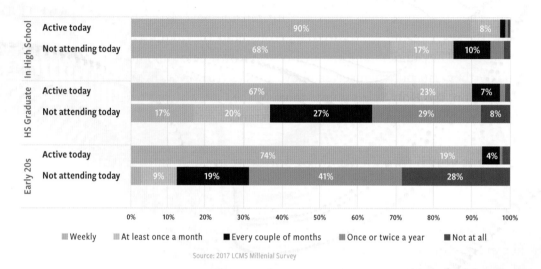

Source: 2017 LCMS Millenial Survey

As young people transition out of high school and onto the next steps, the resilience of their faith gets tested. The biggest drop-off in worship attendance for those who leave the church happens right after high school graduation. It isn't a surprise to those involved with youth ministry that this is a difficult transition to navigate. This time can often be several transitions in one. It may take many connections to help ensure a young adult has transitioned well into whatever is next in his or her life.

We often see this when a young adult has moved and struggles to look for a new church, especially if he or she has grown up in one congregation. As Julianna wrote in chapter 3, visiting a new church can be difficult. There can be differences between the congregation that lovingly brought them Word and Sacrament ministry their whole lives and a new church. Young people may mourn the loss of relationships that for so long had come naturally. Even small things like poor signage, a website that hasn't been updated, or a lack of general welcome can make it difficult for young people to visit again or find another congregation to visit.

This is one of the areas where we see seven practices overlap. Healthy congregations should have warmth, challenge, and grace for young people who are visiting. This environment can make all the difference as young adults transition into a new place. Likewise, young people must also know the value of the Christian Church. As they do, they will give congregations grace and second tries, even after an initial visit may have been difficult. It will encourage them to keep trying until they find a church home and not let other distractions get in the way.

Resilient youth can build relationships with people who are different from them.

Mark remembers his parents preparing him to go off to public school kindergarten. It wasn't just one conversation but an ongoing one about how a young Lutheran Christian was to work hard, make new friends, and behave for his teachers and other adults. It was to be done out of appreciation for all God had provided him.

"You should behave better for Mrs. Kyle than you do for us. She is God's gift to you, teaching you in ways we can't and allowing you to meet new friends."

"Love all your classmates like Jesus loves you. Be kind."

"You will invite all your boy classmates to your birthday party. Even the ones who may annoy you will get an invitation."

"You will go to every boy birthday party you are invited to. Do not 'lose' the invite."

"There are kids in your class that don't have all you have. Help them and look out for them."

"Don't take yourself and life too seriously, and have fun with other kids."

"Obey your teachers and principal. Be a good example to others."

"You are going to encounter lots of new things. We are always here to talk, and you can always use us as an excuse to get out of troubling situations."

Along with other words of love and support, Mark's parents reflected well Jesus' final teachings to His disciples in John 13–17 and the tension that Christians are in the world but not of the world. They modeled and spoke Law and Gospel continually as they prepared Mark for what he would face in school and in the future. Being the third of three children, Mark knew his parents prayed a lot and had learned some lessons too.

It was impressed on Mark that his Baptism makes him different. As salt and light in the world, he had opportunities to shine the light of Jesus to others and share hope. This light shining was done in relationships with others. One of Mark's favorite Sunday School songs, "Jesus Loves the Little Children," was about to get real-life application. Mark wishes he could tell you he behaved well and could share stories of his great piety. He wishes he could honestly say he shared Jesus with every hurting friend, loved well, and worked hard. But he didn't. Sin, idolatry, and the philosophy of the world won out over God's Word. However, in the middle of his failings, the Holy Spirit granted strength to serve well and resist temptation. A strong family, a great church, great teachers, and great friends helped mold Mark into being that kind of person as he learned to love others and face adversity.

Mark's parents prepared him well for the "real world," if only yet in kindergarten. He would learn to love other people, some with quite different backgrounds, beliefs, attitudes, and behaviors. He would also have to learn how to guard himself from harm. Whether parents homeschool or send kids to Lutheran school, private school, or public school, their kids will be blessed with opportunities to be salt and light. They should also be prepared to face challenges to their faith.

Generation Z and Generation Alpha experience even more diversity today. They experience diverse ethnicities, philosophies, socioeconomic statuses, and more in society. Engaging the world will quickly open their eyes to both the loving diversity created by God and the effects of sin, temptation, and worldviews not in alignment with God's Word. These differences can be a bit dangerous. However, resilient and well-supported young people who are prepared can stand strong amid the challenges of the world.

Many teens in your youth ministry may not know Lutherans outside of their congregation. If they have friends who are Christian, they may be from other denominations. Resilient youth embrace the diversity of our world and appreciate the breadth of God's family. They need to understand the difference between Christian denominations, but it is also good for them to appreciate the support they may find from other Christian friends in secular settings.

As the number of young people who claim no religious affiliation grows, it is impossible for a teen today not to have at least some relationship with peers who are not Christian. Some of these relationships will be with friends, teammates, or coworkers. Others will be para-social relationships with influencers or people they connect with via technology. Even if most of their friends are Christians, they have technology that can show them a variety of worldviews in a short amount of time. This exposure to different thoughts and beliefs isn't always bad, especially if the young person has developed resilience.

Teens are in an odd phase where they may have little control over whom they spend time with. They do not choose who is in their classes. They may have limited job, sports, or activity options. In fact, they may often be interacting more with those of different faiths and beliefs than many adults do. By God's grace, resilient Christians take the questions, new ideas, and struggles back through the filter of their baptismal faith and truth known in God's Word.

Parents and supportive adults should be in continued conversation with youth as they develop relationships that test their resilience. Open communication helps keep adults checked in to questions, concerns, and doubts. It also allows adults to step in with tools for resilience and even be prepared to help them end a relationship that might push them outside of what their resilience can manage. As teens mature, they have deeper roots and can handle more pressure. As this happens, conversations can turn toward future transitions, vocations, and relationships, like marriage, friends, and business partnerships.

Resilient youth can navigate disagreements in a humble, loving way.

Gender and sexuality, mental health, abortion, reaching unbelievers, and personal faith. These were the top five topics youth said they wished the church would talk about more in our polling at the 2022 LCMS Youth Gathering. All of these topics bring with them some form of disagreement. Even faithful Christians may disagree on these difficult topics. Yet God has given us His Word, both of Law and Gospel, for our good as we engage in difficult topics together.

GENDER AND SEXUALITY, MENTAL HEALTH, ABORTION, REACHING UNBELIEVERS, AND PERSONAL FAITH. THESE WERE THE TOP FIVE TOPICS YOUTH SAID THEY WISHED THE CHURCH WOULD TALK ABOUT MORE IN OUR POLLING AT THE 2022 LCMS YOUTH GATHERING.

While youth leaders might be inclined to avoid controversial topics, youth are looking for answers. They are on the front line of a changing world. No matter how youth leaders and parents try to avoid it, teens will be put into situations where they need to defend what they believe with humble confidence. Involvement in youth ministry can be a time that helps teens dig deep roots and find truth in God's Word.

Through the Holy Spirit, resilient youth navigate disagreements in a way that fosters relationships while pointing to the truth of the Gospel. This starts with

> YOUTH MINISTRY CAN BE A TIME THAT HELPS TEENS DIG DEEP ROOTS AND FIND TRUTH IN GOD'S WORD.

learning to listen well and ask good questions. If we want to be humble and loving, we first have to understand clearly what other people are trying to say. After listening to them, we can help youth engage in critical thinking about how best to respond to the situation. This process is going to be different from topic to topic, but it should always give everyone involved patience and respect. One of the most important things teens can learn to do in disagreements is to offer up confession and absolution freely. We are going to make mistakes when we disagree and hurt those with whom we are trying to build a relationship. Knowing we will fail and that God will provide us forgiveness gives us confidence to approach hard topics again.

Disagreements with others on issues of theology may require continued conversation rather than a onetime debate. It is important to remind teens that in humble confidence, we don't have to use guilt or manipulation to convince someone what we believe is true. Resilient youth aren't just looking for a "win." Instead, they trust in the work of the Holy Spirit to give them words and to work in the hearts of others.

Part of being people of warmth, challenge, and grace is not letting conflict slide but rather addressing it lovingly. Teens will need assistance in developing the skills to do this well. Helping them understand Law and Gospel is difficult but important work. We can help them find Law and Gospel in God's Word and then teach them how to speak it in love while balancing both. Even experienced adults will struggle with this. We teach and walk alongside youth as they learn new ways to express what we know to be true in God's Word.

It can be helpful to find ways to practice managing conflict in families and youth ministry so that when conflict arises elsewhere, youth can be confident in talking about sin and broken relationships rather than trying to overlook it. Congregations and families are teaching young people how to handle disagreements in their world by how they handle disagreements internally. In our moment of sharing challenge and grace, both youth and adults can recognize we overcome conflict only by the grace of God and through the work of the Holy Spirit.

A well-known bumper sticker or sign has a phrase along the lines of "God says it. I believe it. That settles it." While this sentiment can sometimes cause indigestion because it sounds like it is not willing to invite discussions or conversations, there is also a beauty to the statement. As we wrote in the 40 End Goals, "This fallen world will bring tough topics and issues. God's Holy Word gives me answers and responses to these topics. I may at times struggle with these answers, but God's Word and promises are enough." We want young people to hunger deeply to understand what Scripture says and to understand what the church for centuries has believed and confessed. When they have real struggles, resiliency helps them hold tight to God's Word and hold it as the only place to look for truth. It's important to support and prepare youth for disagreements with someone who has authority over them. Youth may already face situations with teachers, bosses, and coaches who have different beliefs, and priorities, or exhibit sinful behavior. These situations stretch youth's thinking about holding to their faith while respecting authority. They may need to consider how their actions and words witness to Jesus. The Bible provides great accounts like Joseph and Daniel to help a young person explore these situations and consider how to act. Also, they can constantly be reminded of Jesus' forgiveness as they try to faithfully serve in their vocations.

Resilient youth are lifelong learners who face doubt and challenge by turning to God's Word.

One of the very first acts of what would become the Walther League in 1875 was to purchase a bookcase and a set of books creating their first lending library. In the second convention of the Walther League, leaders committed to publishing a newsletter that would have articles of history and theology to help educate their members.[22] They believed that the more resources that were available to young people, the more confident they would be to face their ever-changing world. While the target audience of those books was a touch older than our high school youth, the same may be said today. We have many more tools available today than at the turn of the last century, but the strategy to equip youth with resources to feed their deep roots still holds.

> RESILIENT YOUTH KNOW THERE WILL ALWAYS BE SOMETHING NEW TO LEARN IN GOD'S LIVING AND ACTIVE WORD.

Resilient youth know there will always be something new to learn in God's living and active Word. Just as the world, sin, and the devil will continually seek to throw doubt at us and challenge us, youth can be confident that by returning to Scripture, to worship, and to the community of believers, we can learn something new. God is always giving us the gifts of faith, wisdom, and new understanding through His Word. At each age and life

---

22 For more information on Walther League, see Pahl, *Hopes and Dreams of All*.

circumstance, lifelong learners know the simple message of God's love and forgiveness given to us through Jesus needs to be on their minds and lips.

Youth ministry develops this kind of resilient youth by connecting them to skills for lifelong learning. This includes not just understanding the Bible but knowing how to use tools like footnotes, concordances, and maps. It can mean introducing them to the Small and Large Catechisms as well as other books that might help them dig deeper into specific topics. There are a number of tools that can be put in a young person's arsenal to help him or her face doubt and challenge.

Youth leaders may sometimes underestimate the capacity of young people. Instead of choosing to paraphrase or read texts to teens, have them read the passage themselves out loud. Encourage them to have a regular Bible they will read, highlight, and put notes into, even if it is on an app. Expose them to bigger theological texts and see what engagement you might get. While not every youth is going to be ready to take on the difficult language in parts of the Book of Concord, some teens want that kind of challenge. Practice diving deep into theology that interests them, showing them skills for biblical investigation along the way.

In the more than thirty years since the first LCMS youth poll, the number of times youth have responded to questions of faith with "I don't know" has increased tremendously. This is especially true when it comes to issues of faith like women's ordination, gender and sexuality, and more. Young people are facing challenges to their baptismal faith in different ways than previous generations. They will have new experiences and information that may make them question what they have read in God's Word or question the church's interpretation. Today, before youth deem Scripture as wrong or irrelevant, we hope for an attitude that will first have them return to the Word of God and study and pray for the Holy Spirit to work in their hearts and minds.

As we wrote in the opening to this set of practices, middle and high school students are learning to formulate arguments, developing an understanding of nuance and empathy, and beginning to push for independence. Teachers will likely see this as a challenge or apathy. While it may be frustrating at times, this is also why so many youth leaders love this age. In fact, this challenge can help youth leaders dive deeper and grow in their own understanding as they teach teens to be lifelong learners.

When young people push back, there is an opportunity to help them think through difficult issues in Scripture. As you teach, it is helpful to build space for meaningful discussion. Allow time for them to ask their questions, even if it comes across as a challenge or less than a fully formed idea. Treat their questions seriously, even the slightly silly ones. Show them that God has gifted us with an understanding of Him in the Bible that can carry us through any tough questions or circumstances.

Many youth leaders today remember times when a pastor, church worker, or supportive adult was patient and engaged in answering their many questions. They reflect now to see how these discussions helped foster their life of faith. Often the questions that youth leaders most want to dismiss as off-topic or unimportant are the ones that lead us to the more important questions. Taking a teen's faith exploration seriously often pays dividends beyond what we can see.

During Julianna's coursework to become a director of Christian education, she found herself in a class that was discussing how to handle difficult questions of faith with youth. The professor posed a challenging question to the class and asked students how they would respond if a teen had approached them with that question. With far too much confidence, Julianna responded that she would simply say she didn't know. After all, wasn't it okay for us to admit that there were limits to our knowledge and that there are mysteries in Christ we may never understand?

That professor stood right by Julianna and simply responded, "You can do better than 'I don't know.'" This sparked an important conversation. The answer to some of our faith questions, including some serious ones, is that Christians simply do not know. We cannot understand all the mysteries of Christ. Our limited minds do not work like God's, and that is a gift rather than a stumbling block. There are times when the leader may need to talk seriously about the limits of our understanding. In these moments, youth leaders can point youth back to God's promises and faithfulness in which we are certain through faith.

There are other times when a deeper understanding or even an answer can be found for a teen. In leaning into those difficult questions, youth leaders model how to be lifelong learners. Young people learn that they don't have to check their intellect out to have faith in God. As we help young people understand their faith, it is vital to recognize when we are faced with a God much bigger than us and when we can be more deeply enlightened by the Holy Spirit.

But If Not . . .

Shadrach, Meshach, and Abednego were young men when they were serving King Nebuchadnezzar. They were God's people who were exiled to Babylon. As the Israelites, including Daniel, worked to stay true to their faith, they found challenges that threatened their lives. Nebuchadnezzar had created a golden image of himself and wished everyone to bow down before it. While this is clearly idolatry, the pressure to join in worship just to get by had to have been tremendous. It would have been far easier to slip into sin, bow, and make sure they could live another day.

Shadrach, Meshach, and Abednego were not unlike young people today who are facing pressures all around them to bow down to much more deceptive idols. Young people today are in a culture that often works in opposition to their faith. They are asked all day every day to bow down to the gods of social media likes, achievement, success, and money. While it is easier to bow down to these idols, a resilient identity in Christ challenges them to withstand such pressure.

In Daniel 3:16–18, Shadrach, Meshach, and Abednego say, "O Nebuchadnezzar, we have no need to answer you in this matter. If this be so, our God whom we serve is able to deliver us from the burning fiery furnace, and He will deliver us out of your hand, O king. But if not, be it known to you, O king, that we will not serve your gods or worship the golden image that you have set up." They knew God was able to save them from the certain death of the furnace, and they trusted that God would love and protect them.

When we talk about resilience, the third sentence is key. "But if not . . ." tells us that even if God didn't come through exactly as they hoped, that wouldn't change the faith they had in Him. "But if not . . ." shows us that even when faced with the most extraordinary pressure, they trusted their identity in God enough to not back down. "But if not . . ." says that even in the face of death, they believed that God would fulfill His promises.

God can work in youth to produce a "But if not" kind of resilience. Teens can face all kinds of difficulties and come out the other side with a greater, deeper understanding of their baptismal faith and their identity in Christ. Youth ministry can help them know who they are in Christ with so much certainty that they are able to call sin out, even if it risks popularity, future opportunities, or even death. Parents and supportive adults can stand alongside youth in those moments with humble confidence. In doing so, youth ministry leaders demonstrate how the whole church is with them as they seek to serve the one true God.

It isn't easy. In fact, it might lead them into the fire. Shadrach, Meshach, and Abednego were saved by God, not from the fire but in it. They went all the way into that furnace trusting that God was with them. As they did, they were able to show God's power to all who witnessed it. That same God is with us and all teens now. Whether teens are in the fire now, facing the fire with fear or confidence, or standing firm supporting others, our God is giving them faith and holding them fast so that they, too, might witness mightily what our God can do.

DISCUSSION QUESTIONS

1. How would you describe how deeply rooted and resilient you are in your faith? How would you describe your youths' resiliency?

2. How are you navigating disagreements in youth ministry? How can you use these disagreements to model and teach how to have disagreements in a humble and loving way?

3. When have you experienced resistance while sharing the Gospel? How can that experience help as an example (good or bad) for teens?

4. How does your youth ministry and its leaders prepare youth for the trials of life, including life-altering situations or a crisis? How can youth leaders prepare for God to use them to keep youth rooted in God's baptismal promises?

5. List some of the transitions youth and young adults are going through. How can a congregation provide resources and prepare young people for these transitions, especially those that regularly happen, like the beginning of college or career life?

6. How are you modeling and teaching youth to be lifelong learners who face doubt and challenge by turning to God's Word? What are some skills you might want to practice with them?

SEVEN PRACTICES IN PRACTICE:

Develop a Resilient Identity in Christ

We talked with Heidi Lewis about how she helps foster a resilient identity in Christ with her youth and congregation. Heidi is a director of Christian education who has served parishes in Colorado, Texas, Mississippi, and Missouri. She has served a variety of age groups and congregations including suburban, urban, and church plants. She loves Jesus and kids. She is blessed with a mission planter husband and a grace bomb of a daughter.

What are some challenges you see that affect the faith lives of young people?

The biggest attack to resiliency right now is around identity and who you are. There doesn't seem to be any understanding in culture of what truth is, and God's truth is being challenged left and right. When truth, especially the truth of God, is questioned, it can shake the foundation of who you are.

The philosophies around youth are so counter to the Gospel, and they are listening to music, taking in screen time, and going to school hearing them. It can be challenging to be a positive, Christ-centered voice for youth.

How does your ministry help youth face challenges to their faith?

Our congregation has adopted this hallmark or battle cry for our spiritual lives. It came from Pastor Joel Christiansen from another nearby church. We say, "Baptized child of God, you are loved by the Father. You are led by the Spirit, and you belong to Jesus and no one else." We repeat that over and over. We refer to that statement as we teach and remind young people of that truth often.

We even give a pillowcase from the church that has the phrase on it when they join or there is a Baptism. We talk about how we rest knowing these things are true and we rise each day propelled with that as our purpose. So when they get an overbearing coach who says, "You belong to me," they can know they belong to Jesus. Or if they get into an abusive relationship, they can know the truth about who they are even if that person tells you otherwise.

What are some ways you support young people who experience a crisis?

I think back to when I was in crisis as a youth. I was sixteen when I had two close friends who were in a terrible car accident that ultimately took their lives. Soon after I was on a backpacking trip with my youth group, but I separated myself from the group. My counselor followed me as I sat by a tree crying and sat with me. I don't know what she said, but I know that she was there.

When kids are going through a crisis, the ministry of presence is powerful. If they start stepping away from the community after a crisis, go after them. You don't have to have the words. You can just be there and walk alongside them. Your presence can show them they are loved, even if you don't have all the answers. You don't always get to decide what a crisis is for a teen. It might be a bad grade or the death of a grandparent. It might be a school shooting that happens in another community. Show up and remind them of their identity in Christ, that they are loved and have purpose.

What are some transitions you see in teens' lives? How do you support them in those transitions?

The transition from elementary school to middle school is getting harder because we are asking kids to grow up so much faster. Other transitions from middle school to high school and from high school to college are big moments as well. There may be transitions with people moving in and out of their homes, like stepparents, grandparents, or siblings. There is even a transition when youth first gain access to the internet. It doesn't seem like a big rite of passage, but it can be difficult to navigate.

To support them well, I should be doing life with them before that transition. Otherwise, I might not know about it. Creating a relationship with them allows me to speak truth centered on the Gospel. If I'm not already doing that before the transition, I am going to seem like an intruder, and they are more likely to reject what I say. Our community needs to have joy because experiencing joy helps set a good foundation for support as well. For me as a leader, I want to empower other leaders to help support transitions as well. This doesn't have to be just adults but peers and older adults who are immersed in God's Word and Spirit-led to serve and walk alongside young people.

Young people are going to disagree with other Christians or with those who believe differently. How do you prepare young people for those disagreements?

We must wrap our kids in God's Word and robust apologetics. If we want them to make a stand, they have to have a solid foundation. The culture will not give them enough to stand on. They have to be ready with a deep understanding of what they believe. We also can't rescue our kids all the time. We need to let them be strong on their own and grow spiritual grit.

How do you help support young people to be lifelong learners?

I do that by humbly modeling it myself. I am honest about how I am still learning. We talk about how God's Word is solid and unchangeable but also so rich and alive that we can learn from it every day. When I am talking with kids or teaching a class, I will say, "Oh, I just learned that this week." It's important to have humility and not pretend you know it all. Be willing to look for answers with them as you grow together.

Chapter 10

LIVE OUT THEIR UNIQUE VOCATION

Highs and lows. It is a staple opener of youth ministries across the country. As teens come in and get settled for Bible study or prayer, the leader will ask everyone to share something that was great about his or her week and something that was difficult or disappointing. This simple interaction engages everyone in sharing and learning. It also gives youth leaders insight into where the youth are emotionally and what activities might be going on in their lives. It is a great tool if you haven't used it before.

One limitation to highs and lows is that it can set an imaginary boundary between our time in youth ministry and the rest of our lives. We ask one youth to talk about what went well and what struggles he or she had during the week, but then we move quickly onto the next person with little response. Once each youth in the circle shares highs and lows, the youth leader may move immediately on to the study, which is disconnected from what was just shared. When this happens, youth can get the sense that the test bombed or the amazing performance in the game Friday night isn't connected to their faith. Teens involved in this activity may subtly sense a separation between church time and the rest of the week.

Youth and adults increasingly struggle with compartmentalizing their faith. As Christianity moves to the margins of our society, there is no pressure to express faith at school or work. In fact, there can be active pushback against it. Families are less church-centric than previous generations. Church may be important, but it is often not the center of our social activities or even our volunteer opportunities. Families can fully engage in worship, prayer, the Bible, and building supportive congregational community from the time they enter the parking lot until the time they leave. Yet the rest of the week, faith is often private. Faith is something they may think about, but it is certainly not something they openly share or discuss.

In Baptism, God gives us faith that should permeate every part of our lives. Deeply understanding our faith and a resilient identity in Christ are critical goals for youth, but vocation helps them bring their faith out into the world. Vocation is God's calling for His human creatures to serve their neighbor and care for His creation through their unique roles and tasks. Young people who live out their unique vocations are empowered by the Holy Spirit to make every single activity of their week a chance to share Jesus' love and care for God's creation. Unique vocation fights back against compartmentalization of faith, which is only personal. Vocation means that no part of our week, neither the highs nor the lows, is separate from our faith.

> IN BAPTISM, GOD GIVES US FAITH THAT SHOULD PERMEATE EVERY PART OF OUR LIVES.

Vocation does more than bring faith into everyday life. It also gives what we do purpose. Teens are asking big questions about identity and future goals. As they do, they want to find meaning in what they do. They ask the question "why?" a lot. While it might sound like whining to some adults, it is often a question of purpose. They want to know how to prioritize their life when they become independent adults. They might prioritize pleasing friends, family, or teachers too much. They may make their decisions based on likes and follows, money, or whatever seems like the least amount of work. Vocation helps them see that their actions are made by God to serve others.

As youth begin to understand the needs of the world, they can become overwhelmed. Teens will often become incredibly passionate about areas of need and concern in our world. These big issues can be powerful catalysts for living out vocation. They can also lead teens to become disheartened when they see the limitations of what they alone can do. Vocation, however, is not lived out alone. All of God's people have callings through Baptism. Even when young people want to change the world, having divine purpose gives us a fresh perspective and renewed energy for what we can do today. When we all do small tasks, God can make big things happen. God is at work in and through many people who are all caring for God's creation together. Their contributions are noticed and appreciated as they work alongside the whole Body of Christ.

Each week is going to be filled with highs and lows, even if we don't ask about them during Bible study. But if we are pushing toward these discipleship goals, all they experience will be seen in the light of their faith. Teens find ways to share the Gospel with others, serve and lead in their congregation and community, and see all their daily activities as a chance to show warmth, challenge, and grace to a world in need of the Gospel.

What Is Vocation?

If we want youth to live out their unique vocation, we must first understand what that means. Usually, the word *vocation* is associated with the work we do to earn a living or manage our household. While jobs and careers are a part of vocation, the theology of vocation encompasses much more than just work.

Vocation comes from the Latin word *vocatio*, meaning "calling." In Martin Luther's time, the concept of vocation was limited to those who were serving the church in particular roles: priest, nun, monk, and so on. People in these roles dedicated their entire life to the church, and the church recognized only these as divine callings or vocations. Luther believed this limited the way vocation is described in Scripture. The Bible says all baptized children of God are set apart for holy work. As the priesthood of all believers, everyone who is baptized has a calling to serve God by loving our neighbors in His name.

The theology of vocation says that God cares for creation and serves us through His baptized children. God did not just create and then walk away. Instead, God uses His people, who are empowered by the Holy Spirit, to care for and love the world. Every good thing we do for our church, family, or neighbor we do because God is acting through us. A. Trevor Sutton says it this way in *Being Lutheran: Living in the Faith You Have Received*: "God works through normal, everyday people doing normal, everyday tasks. God calls normal, everyday Christians to live out their faith as wives, husbands, mothers, fathers, workers, bosses, church members, and citizens. Luther referred to these vocations as the 'masks of God.' Although it appears that the farmer works to provide grain, it is actually God working through farmer to provide daily bread."[23]

> THE THEOLOGY OF VOCATION SAYS THAT GOD CARES FOR CREATION AND SERVES US THROUGH HIS BAPTIZED CHILDREN.

God calls His baptized children to love Him and serve their neighbor. As we talk about vocation, we often use metaphorical language like the masks of God or God's hands and feet. While they might seem a bit confusing at times, these images help us remember that God is the one doing the acting, not us. God could care for creation in a lot of ways, but He chooses to use us. In fact, God created each of us unique and placed us where we are so that we can love others in His name.

Vocation is not something done to earn salvation. It is not an obligation or a way to guilt your youth into carrying their faith out into the world. It is something we do because we have been so deeply loved, as 1 John 4:9, 11 says: "In this the love of God was made manifest among us, that God sent His only Son into the world, so that we might live through Him. . . . Beloved, if God so loved us, we also ought to love one another."

We talk less directly or frequently about the theology of vocation than other aspects of our faith. As we share about the seven practices, vocation is often the

---

23 A. Trevor Sutton, *Being Lutheran: Living in the Faith You Have Received* (St. Louis: Concordia Publishing House, 2016), 212.

one youth leaders feel least equipped to discuss. As a result, parents and adult leaders may not have ever stopped to consider their own vocations. If we are to help young people live out their unique vocation, we first must consider ours.

Youth leaders, parents, church workers, pastors, and other supportive adults should be attentive to their unique vocations. To effectively meet this goal, adults must be willing to do self-reflection on their gifts, skills, experience, and passions. As you read more about vocation in this chapter, take time to be self-reflective on your vocational roles. As you become more aware of how God is using you as His hands and feet, you will be better equipped to walk alongside youth as they do the same.

Youth understand their role as Christ's hands and feet in their church, home, community, and other areas of vocation.

We can break down the broader theology of vocation into smaller pieces to help us convey it to youth. Vocation is thought of in three "estates":

Church

Home

Community

Each estate encompasses some part of our lives and contains multiple vocations. As a member of a congregation, you may have a role as a youth leader, as well as a supportive adult, sermon listener, musician, or usher. The estate of home includes both those in your household and the vocations that do or will support your household, like work or school. Vocations in your community include neighbor, supporter of local businesses, volunteer, or voter. One place you can find many vocations and what they are called to do is the often overlooked Table of Duties in *Luther's Small Catechism with Explanation.*

While it doesn't encompass everything, it can be helpful to have youth consider their roles, responsibilities, and relationships in each of the estates. Sometimes seeing their unique vocations can seem a bit abstract for teens. Breaking their callings down further into roles, responsibilities, and relationships helps identify the regular ways they are sharing God's love and caring for neighbors. It also helps them see just how many ways God is using them as His hands and feet right now.

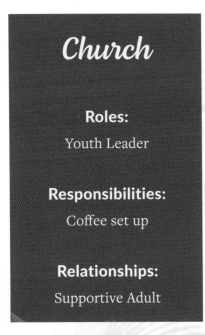

Church

Roles:
Youth Leader

Responsibilities:
Coffee set up

Relationships:
Supportive Adult

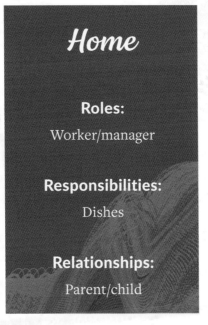

Home

Roles:
Worker/manager

Responsibilities:
Dishes

Relationships:
Parent/child

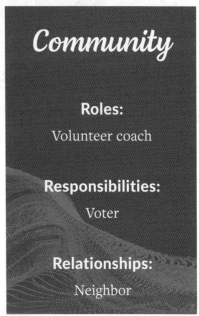

Community

Roles:
Volunteer coach

Responsibilities:
Voter

Relationships:
Neighbor

Gen Z is action-orientated and achievement driven. According to Barna, Gen Z's academic and work achievements and hobbies are more important to their identity than their friends, families, and even religious life.[24] They were more likely than any other generation to say that they often define their skills and giftings—what they do or what they are good at.[25] In many ways, Gen Z identifies who they are by what they do. In the same way, they are looking at Christians and the church and identifying them by what they choose to do or not do. Beyond wanting to deeply understand their baptismal faith, they want to see faith in action. The theology of vocation helps them bridge what they believe and their actions.

Teens who are action-oriented may grasp onto vocation with both hands. Living out and sacrificing for our faith helps us keep apathy at bay and shows teens that what they do today matters. God uses our ordinary work to accomplish great things, even on the smallest of scales. Luther says, "For He will be working all things through you; He will milk the cow through you and perform the most servile duties through you, and all the greatest and least duties alike will be pleasing to Him."[26]

Teens who are achievement driven tend to be focused on the future. They have their eyes on what's next, including adult independence. While striving for

---

24 The Barna Group, *Gen Z*, vol. 1 (Ventura, CA: The Barna Group, 2018), 41.

25 "Gen Z Are Leaning into Their Gifts—Will the Church Help?" The Barna Group (website), January 5, 2022, https://www.barna.com/research/gen-z-gifts/ (accessed March 13, 2023).

26 Martin Luther, *Luther's Works*, vol. 6 (St. Louis: Concordia Publishing House, 1955), 10.

excellence is good, they need the right focus on Jesus. They may believe vocation is tied to work or future roles and responsibilities. Teaching vocation helps them slow down and focus more on today. God doesn't need them to complete a degree, become the captain of the team, be married, or own a home before their vocational call starts. Youth have important vocations now. Rather than focusing on their achievement, vocation helps ground them in God as the source of all good things.

Teaching vocation helps calm nerves and give confidence about the future. Many of us can remember how difficult it was to find our future direction as we approached high school graduation. In vocation, whatever decision they pursue, God will be with them. It expands the career tracks or degrees youth can follow. Even if they fail to accomplish what they hope, the Holy Spirit will still be with them, giving them new vocations to live out. Teens can take the pressure off themselves to make the future happen and place it on God.

Teens may be involved in many activities in school and in their communities. They may change jobs or extracurriculars seasonally. This means that their roles and responsibilities will also change regularly. Rather than avoiding teaching vocation, youth leaders can use these transitional times for youth as an opportunity to help youth navigate how it feels to change vocation through phases of life. While some vocational roles, especially within our family relationships, are more constant, it is important to help youth understand and prepare for vocations to change through different phases of life.

Youth reach out to their neighbor in word and deed to love and share the Good News of Jesus.

While much of youth ministry may focus on teens in our congregations, there are teens in our communities and across the world who need to hear the Gospel. As noted earlier in this book, Generation Z has the highest rate of religious unaffiliation of any generation. Our goal is for youth to live out their unique vocations, including sharing the Gospel in word and deed with those who do not believe.

In Luke 10, Jesus sends out seventy-two believers to go into towns ahead of Him. He says, "The harvest is plentiful, but the laborers are few. Therefore pray earnestly to the Lord of the harvest to send out laborers into His harvest. Go your way; behold, I am sending you out as lambs in the midst of wolves" (vv. 2–3).

Jesus asks them to look for people of peace who will listen to the Good News. Our youth can do the same thing. As they live out their vocation, they will find people who are open and receptive to hearing about what they believe. Our goal is that they feel confident in engaging these people over time so that as the Holy Spirit works, those around them may be drawn closer to Jesus. We can help youth meet this goal by practicing sharing their stories of God's work as well as stories from Scripture. Youth leaders can take time to help investigate questions they get from peers and create programmatic opportunities for them to invite friends who might be interested. It is good to remind youth that this is often easier said than done. Sharing the Gospel can be hard for adults, even those with more understanding and resilient faith than youth. Yet each time we share with someone receptive to the Gospel, we trust God is using us.

There are also times when Jesus warns that those going out in His name will not be welcomed. This is also a difficult truth for teens. Youth may hesitate to share what they believe with a diverse group of friends or family because they are unsure of how that might impact their relationships. Poorly done evangelism strategies have been called out often enough that youth already know some of the pitfalls. Young people today are often hesitant to say or do something that might alienate or marginalize someone else or themselves. Older adults will need to listen well to concerns and give encouragement as they go.

It is important to remind both adults and young people that they are not responsible for creating faith. The Holy Spirit is with them, giving them the right words and working in the hearts of others. Someone else's faith doesn't depend on them. People are not projects that we take on until we convince them of faith. Regardless of how we treat people, we are going to fail to love our neighbor as ourselves. Youth are simply called to share who they know God to be and who God has made them to be in Christ.

Teens should be concerned about others who don't know Jesus because we believe we have hope and salvation in Jesus alone. If youth leaders share that concern for the eternal lives of others, adults should also model what it looks like to share the Gospel as they love their neighbor in word and deed. Whether they are asking or not, youth are wondering if youth leaders, parents, pastors, and church workers really believe what they teach. It is hard to teach them to share the Gospel when we insulate our circle of relationships to Christians only. One way we encourage sharing the Gospel is by modeling how important it is by sharing it with people in our lives as well.

When we share the Gospel, we might be planting a seed that we will not get a chance to see grow. Youth who share the Gospel may never see their friends change their beliefs, but they should know God is at work. Teens can get up and try again, knowing that (to paraphrase Luther's sentiment) "God does not need our good works, but our neighbor does."[27]

Healthy youth ministry can help young people engage in not only conversations about difficult issues with the people around them but in unique vocations to serve others. Young people may be passionate about caring for their neighbor but see the church as unresponsive or inactive. Youth ministries should be prepared to help young people reach out in faith toward others, even if it makes them uncomfortable.

Mark remembers an example of a possible missed opportunity at a church workers conference he attended. The organizers of the event did something bold but helpful. They asked young adults who grew up in the LCMS but had since left the LCMS or the Christian faith to address the audience about their insight on retention. One young man discussed how as a youth he had an interest in serious current events such as war and governmental injustice in our world. He felt his questions about these topics were ignored by the church. He also said there was little support as he considered careers that used these passions. Mark wonders if a pastor, youth leader, or supportive adult would have encouraged or engaged this young man differently, then his story of lost faith wouldn't have happened.

This young man was passionate about caring for the world. Unfortunately, he felt that the church did not see this as his vocation. While he continued to follow those interests and desires, even caring for others, he did so without the church, losing his identity in Christ along the way. Youth leaders can learn a lesson to help use the empathy and passion young people have for service to engage them deeply rather than discourage them.

Youth serve and lead in their congregation and community.

Healthy youth ministries give opportunities to serve and lead. Yet when we talk to youth leaders, they are frustrated that those opportunities often go unfilled. Teens and their families often have busy schedules that run from early in the morning until late at night. It can seem like the only time teens take advantage of

---

27 Gustaf Wingren, *Luther on Vocation*, trans. Carl C. Rasmussen (Eugene, OR: Wipf and Stock Publishers, 1957), 10.

service or leadership opportunities is when it is an obligation for school, a scholarship, or as part of preparing for larger youth events. Just as we encourage youth to prioritize faith practices, we can help them prioritize this service as part of their vocation as well.

Julianna remembers a time when her congregation was struggling to get help decorating for the different seasons of the Church Year. This job required dusty, heavy lifting and an understanding of how pieces like large Christmas trees with prestrung lights go together. For many years, it was done by faithful older servants in the church. When the nature of the work became an issue for these older servants, two things helped her engage extra youth and their families to come assist. First was helping them see that they had unique skills (in this case energy and muscles) that other people in the congregation didn't have. Second was reminding them of the bigger picture of what this service did. It helped celebrate Jesus and was a message to those who drove past the church of our celebration of Jesus. And doughnuts, so maybe that's three things.

Helping them to see service as less of an obligation and more of an opportunity can help shift priorities for teens and their families. It is important that our opportunities are tuned to what they are uniquely qualified to do. Understanding vocation provides youth an opportunity to serve and lead together as the Body of Christ. It is a chance to care for your community. Youth leaders can help teens see the bigger purpose of service and leadership as an act and gift from God, though it takes time and intention to help communicate these well.

We know that not every teen is going to be willing or able to join a congregation's opportunities at every time or stage. Just like with adults, there are going to be seasons where schedules or transitions won't allow the time needed for service and leadership. There will also be times when the opportunities available don't fit the teens well. It is important to be patient through these times and give chances to step in for small portions of projects in order to help youth stay connected. As we have said before, sometimes you take the long view on raising up young people to greater levels of service.

Youth are also more likely to engage in service and leadership when it fits their experience, passion, and skills. As parents and supportive adults get to know a young person, they are able to orient them to places God has uniquely gifted them to serve. Teaching vocation, like offering opportunities to serve and lead, can help young people find their unique gifts, skills, passions, and experiences. As youth discover how God has uniquely created them and placed them, they may see more clearly how the Holy Spirit can use them.

AS YOUTH DISCOVER HOW GOD HAS UNIQUELY CREATED THEM AND PLACED THEM, THEY MAY SEE MORE CLEARLY HOW THE HOLY SPIRIT CAN USE THEM.

Helping youth see service and leadership as vocation can give a backdrop to discuss positive and healthy understanding of identity. When young people understand their roles and relationships in light of what God says, it is harder for the world or the devil to get a foothold on who they know they are. Our culture has become highly individualistic. "You do you" emphasizes that everyone should form an identity for themselves and not around God's truth. One's unique vocation speaks to the power of God's gifts to the individual, the passions felt, and the opportunities God has placed before us. We are God's workmanship designed for service to our neighbor.

One of Generation Z's interesting dichotomies is that they are both anxious doing new things because they fear they may do them wrong and they are creative and entrepreneurial problem solvers. Our theology of vocation has beautiful responses to both. First, we don't have to worry about failing in our vocation because it doesn't depend on our work. In our sin, we know we are going to fail. We have confidence that God is going to work, even through our brokenness, to care for the world. Second, it encourages their discipline and excellence while keeping the right focus. Vocation is action by God through us.

Service and leadership can build confidence and develop skills in youth, all while knowing God is at work in and through them. For teens who struggle with a fear of failure, congregational service and leadership can be a place where they have mentors who show warmth, challenge, and grace. When given the opportunity to try new things, teens develop new skills and understanding that will help them in the future. Unlike other high-pressure places, supportive adults and parents can walk through service and leadership with youth as they experience satisfaction and joy in the Christian life.

THE HEART OF VOCATION IS SERVICE. WE SERVE, SHARING THE GOSPEL IN WORD AND DEED, BECAUSE CHRIST FIRST SERVED US.

The heart of vocation is service. We serve, sharing the Gospel in word and deed, because Christ first served us. Youth who are living out their unique vocations are taking opportunities in the church and community to serve and lead consistently now and into the future.

Youth seek to be warm, challenging, and grace-filled to their community and peers.

If you have been reading from the start of the book, the words above will not be a surprise to you. When we considered how young people should approach their vocations, these words came up again. Vocation calls young people out into roles, responsibilities, and relationships. As they gain experiences, our goal is for youth to approach those with the same attitude as the one they see modeled in ministry. An environment of warmth, challenge, and grace modeled by supportive adults who show warmth, challenge, and grace helps raise young people who know how to show warmth, challenge, and grace.

Our current cultural climate tends to move people into "us versus them" stances. We are divided by political affiliations, values, purchasing choices, and even parenting styles. Social media has an algorithm designed to keep users engaged by sharing and affirming their thoughts or creating anger toward others. Rather than being a means of connection, social media has cultivated users who will scroll longer and engage more by creating separate camps. This has spilled out into other media and into our lives.

Seeking to be a person of warmth, challenge, and grace pushes back against those separations. When teens live out these qualities well, they can see artificial dividing lines and untruths for what they are. They can stand firm in what they believe while also seeking to understand those who have different beliefs. Thinking critically about these situations strengthens their own beliefs and helps develop their loving response to those who disagree. Rather than seeking to fight those who are "other," they can pray and act in love.

Outside of the three estates, Luther also talked about the order of Christian love. This additional space for vocation simply reminds us that everyone who is around us is created by God, and our neighbor needs our service. God does not divide people as we do. Instead, God calls us to welcome all, love while giving challenge even when sin is evident, and practice grace as we try to understand one another.

There is a song that perhaps you used to sing in Sunday School called "They'll Know We Are Christians by Our Love." The way young people walk in their world and the type of character they show should distinguish them as Christians. The way they include those on the margins or forgive people who hurt them can point others to Christ. As they grow up into adults, youth who live out their unique vocations will become adult doctors, pastors, teachers, welders, lawyers, civil servants, and documentarians who are all known as Christians by how they show the love of God.

Over time, young people will experience a variety of vocational roles as opportunities and relationships develop and change. In each stage, God continues to call them to share the Gospel and sends the Holy Spirit to make a significant impact through their unique roles. Vocation encourages young people to interact across age groups, belief systems, ability levels, and experiences. In these relationships, they can share God's grace and forgiveness while navigating conflicts and disagreements with truth in love.

Youth are encouraged to pursue church work vocations as it fits their gifts and skills.

Luther helped the church rightly expand its theology of vocation away from only including those in professional church work. Yet vocation does still include those whose gifts, skills, and passion are to serve in this way. There is a shortage of church workers that threatens to only get worse. To reverse this trend, supportive adults and parents should be actively looking for young people who are invested in God's mission who may succeed as pastors, teachers, musicians, administrators, and other full-time church workers.

As you teach vocation, you will find youth with the gifts and temperament for church work. One of the easiest ways to encourage church work is to keep these kinds of positions in front of youth. Talk about them regularly and positively. If you do not already, bring in people who fill some of those roles into your youth ministry program. As teens take an interest, you may want to set up shadow days where they follow a church worker or arrange days to go visit universities that offer church work majors.

Healthy youth ministry can serve as an incubator for future church workers by providing support, encouragement, and foundational training to youth. Some congregations choose to regularly pray for students pursuing church work, particularly calling by name those from their congregation. Others use opportunities to serve and lead as a space to identify and train up those youth who might be a good fit for church work. Opportunities to try out leadership in a congregation can be a great way to help youth investigate professional church work. As you identify youth, take time to point out what you see in them and how that might connect to church work. It might take several conversations as youth consider those possibilities, but it is often the most effective way to encourage youth in this direction.

Even though both Julianna and Mark had church workers as parents, it took other supportive adults to ask questions and encourage them to consider if church work was in their future. Teens who come through your youth ministry may pursue many different careers, and some will have many careers over a lifetime. Helping them see church work careers in a positive light and keeping these options in front of all teens helps God work in their lives and call those who are gifted for that work.

If you currently serve in a church work career as a pastor, director of Christian education, deaconess, or teacher, you can have a major impact on young people who have the gifts and heart to serve in church careers. Your mentoring, invitation to shadow, and honest conversations about the joys and trials of church work give young people the encouragement and confidence to consider serving the church. Church workers who show joy in their roles can help encourage future church workers and give them a positive model of service. And if you haven't been told lately, thank you for letting your light shine!

Avoiding Apathy

One of the biggest shifts in Generation Z and Generation Alpha is that they are generally distrustful of leaders or institutions. Younger generations have seen leaders in many arenas be untrustworthy. They have seen institutions fail the people they claimed to serve. Their consistent exposure to these broken leaders and systems leads to general skepticism. Older generations may be annoyed by this shift, which seems to call into question structures they built or were raised to trust implicitly. Experienced leaders may struggle when young people no longer listen and follow directions without question. Generation Z and Generation Alpha need you to earn your right to speak.

It is no longer sufficient for adult leaders or even parents to simply encourage spiritual practices and living out vocation simply because we say so. We must be ready to talk about why it is important. As we give youth opportunities to serve and lead, they are going to ask many questions and come with some wariness. Experienced leaders should be ready to be honest about success and failure and be clear about purpose. Dismissing their questions or attempts to share their opinions

> IT IS NO LONGER SUFFICIENT FOR ADULT LEADERS OR EVEN PARENTS TO SIMPLY ENCOURAGE SPIRITUAL PRACTICES AND LIVING OUT VOCATION SIMPLY BECAUSE WE SAY SO. WE MUST BE READY TO TALK ABOUT WHY IT IS IMPORTANT.

will only reinforce their skepticism about leaders and institutions.

Generation Z and Generation Alpha are growing up in a world where they hear the brokenness of the church being scrutinized. Youth leaders should be honest about ways that sinners in the church have failed in their vocations. When youth leaders make mistakes, they should be quick to lean into confession and absolution. This reminds youth that God's promises are real and vital for us every day. It also helps set an example that our faith in God is deeply important, not just something taught in a quick twenty-minute lesson that is easily forgotten by the time they get to the car.

In recent years, we have seen a rise in what some call *apatheism*, especially in our teens. *Apatheism* is a term coined for those who believe faith is irrelevant. The question of if God exists doesn't particularly matter because it doesn't seem to have any bearing on life. This is different than atheism, which is when someone actively believes there is no God, or agnosticism, which is when someone actively questions the existence of God. Apatheistic attitudes say that even if I believe in God, it doesn't matter to me, and I don't care about what others may believe.

This is particularly dangerous because it can be difficult to spot in young people. These are youth who are not antagonistic or looking to argue against God. We may see them regularly in church and youth ministry. Yet for them, God simply holds no significance or meaning. They would respond that even if what we teach and preach is true, it doesn't matter to their daily lives. Thus, it doesn't take any priority in their identity or choices. Often, these youth slowly disconnect over time or leave home with no intention of ever looking for another church home.

Youth leaders may need to own some of what leads to apatheism. Youth ministries sometimes actively work to make faith "easy" for youth and families. Expectations are lowered. Programs are full of casual fun in an attempt to keep attendance numbers up. If congregations limit their demands on people's time and fail to challenge them to live out their faith, apatheistic attitudes may result. There are times when engaging a greater audience can help you connect youth to supportive adults or to God's Word. But if we aren't intentionally working toward goals, we may instead teach them that faith in God simply isn't that important.

Challenge in youth ministry means reminding youth consistently that what they believe means something. It may be counterintuitive, but teens want something worth sacrificing for. Many of the other activities they are engaged in make high demands of them, like early practices, late-night rehearsals, and ongoing training.

Shouldn't their spiritual lives demand a lot of them as well?

In His Word, God reminds us that being His children means sacrificing things, being pushed aside, and losing out on what the world says is important. As we read from Luke 10 earlier in this chapter, youth are being sent among wolves. We can't hide that reality from them. Vocation teaches us that our whole lives are not out own but are subject to God. These can be tough teachings. Challenge is not always received well in our church or in our communities. Yet God can use those moments to guide away from apathy and into a deeper faith.

Answering the Big Questions

What am I here on earth to do?

How will I know if I've found success?

What do I want my life to look like after high school?

These questions are a lot more difficult than "What are your highs and lows from this week?" These big questions emerge during adolescence. Youth seek direction, significant relationships, and a chance to impact their communities. They begin to set priorities and long-term goals. They look to parents, extended family, church family, and throughout history for role models of success. In this time of searching, vocation plays an important role in applying their faith and finding their God-given skills.

Even when they are sick of questions about what they plan to do after high school, vocation helps them see how their gifts, skills, passions, and experiences can be used by God. As youth wonder what to do with their lives and how to find success, vocation gives them the lens to see all they do as an opportunity for God to work powerfully. They will begin to see that faith is not just for Sunday mornings but for Tuesday afternoons, Thursday mornings, and every day.

No one's path is going to look the same as others'. We share the same baptismal faith, and the same Holy Spirit gives us resilient identities. Yet we are all made specially and placed specifically by a God who loves us, saves us, and gives us all we need to live out our faith and love others in His name. Teaching vocation answers those big questions, but it doesn't draw a perfect map for youth to follow. Instead, we go forward into whatever is ahead knowing God will go with us.

Teaching vocation provides a place to talk about how one's life has purpose. The almighty God, Creator of the universe, uses us mistake-prone, disagreeable, whiny people to serve others and reflect His glory. It can be alarming how many young people are plagued by hopelessness, worthlessness, and sadness. Teaching vocation can expand how young people see themselves and what they do each day. Helping young people understand how God is using them, or could use them, gives them the courage to try new things, step into new experiences, and engage in new relationships. Where a young person may be invested in unhealthy rhythms or relationships, vocation can give direction and connection.

Those big questions don't go away in adulthood. Parents and supportive adults are also answering those questions for themselves. As life and vocation changes, adults may wonder if their choices have truly led them down the right path. Just like youth, adults wonder if they are making an impact and are having success. Parents, youth leaders, pastors, church workers, and supportive adults all live out critical roles in a young person's life. Our vocations matter not just to us but to the young people in our congregations and communities. We can be assured that our service is a gift from God.

Paul defines it this way: "I have been crucified with Christ. It is no longer I who live, but Christ who lives in me. And the life I now live in the flesh I live by faith in the Son of God, who loved me and gave Himself for me" (Galatians 2:20).

Our goal is for young people to answer those big questions with their understanding of Baptism, their resilient identity in Christ, and their vocation. As God empowers us, this is what we strive to do with every part of youth ministry.

DISCUSSION QUESTIONS

1. What are your vocations? How does God use you in the church, in your home, and in your community to love others and share the Gospel?

2. Are young people encouraged to see how both mundane and extraordinary service are done in honor to God and service to our neighbor?

3. How are you teaching and supporting youth to consider how to reach out to those who don't know Jesus with the Gospel?

4. Would you describe yourself or your youth as warm, challenging, and grace-filled? What can you do to foster those characteristics with God's help?

5. How are you helping youth engage in service and leadership as a part of their vocations?

6. Where do you see apathy in your youth? How can you help them see faith as something worth their time and energy?

7. Who in your ministry might make a good future church worker? How can the congregation encourage them to consider church work as a future vocation?

SEVEN PRACTICES IN PRACTICE:

Congregations will help all young people . . .

To help us get a broader idea of how the congregation plays a role in the final three practices, we talked to Pastor Ben Meyer. Pastor Meyer currently serves at Hope Lutheran Church in Sunbury, Ohio. He is a pastor's kid, a husband, and a father of four children. He enjoys making barbecue in his backyard, making pizza in his kitchen, hiking in the mountains, watching St. Louis Cardinals baseball and Nebraska football, and helping others know Jesus.

How does having young people who live out the final three practices (deeply understand their baptismal faith, develop a resilient identity in Christ, and live out their unique vocation) involved in youth ministry help shape ministry programs?

I don't think that it is any one thing that helps young people to reach this goal, but it's the layered effect of many things.

One thing we do is to use the language of baptismal identity. We don't shy away from using that language because it can actually help shape their thinking. In a world in which youth are encouraged to find their identity in sports, sexuality, grades, race, and any other number of things, we need to remind them of their primary identity in Christ. We need to remind them that God has chosen them and loves them deeply.

Another thing we do when reading Scripture with them is help them to see how it speaks about them and their identity. For instance, if you study 1 Peter 2 with them, you can help them to see that through Baptism into Christ, they are, together with their brothers and sisters in Christ, chosen, set apart, and deeply treasured by God. This helps them to see that it's not merely something we say but something God has said concerning them.

An additional aspect is intentional inclusion of and interaction with adults from the congregation. For instance, once a month, we have what we call "Table Talk," which includes a meal and a topic that we cover. We encourage all ages to participate in these conversations, and it gives our youth an opportunity to interact with, learn from, hear life stories from, and develop relationships with mature adult Christians. These adults are able to share their stories and how they live out their vocations. They have opportunities to share, in a comfortable and conversational way, how Christ has seen them through difficult times. And they are able to express how knowing their identity as a baptized child of God has shaped them and comforted them over the years.

How can supportive adults and parents remind young people what their Baptism means?

Repetition, repetition, repetition. Young people need the constant reminder of who they are in Christ, and there are myriad opportunities for such reminders.

- If you're doing a service day at church, remind them that you're doing this because this is part of what the baptized do.

- When praying with them, include a phrase like, "Since we are Your baptized people."

- When something reminds you of your own Baptism or when a situation arises in which your identity as a baptized child of God is brought to the forefront, talk about that with those young people.

Where do you see a youth's identity in Christ being challenged most today?

Luther wrote in the Large Catechism, "If you could see how many knives, darts, and arrows are every moment aimed at you [Ephesians 6:16], you would be glad to come to the Sacrament as often as possible."[28] Christians facing attacks on their identity in Christ is not a new thing. But youth today face attacks from so many directions. At school, in movies, on social media, and in many other ways, Christians are often portrayed as hateful, unloving, and foolish. Youth are encouraged to look outside of Christ for their identity and to explore in order to "find their true selves."

Sadly, this is a path to increased unhappiness since true joy is found in Christ. But in searching outside of Christ, there is emptiness and endless searching for purpose and identity. Many times, our young people will face the reality that they must either conform or be ostracized.

How do you see the practices deeply understand their baptismal faith, develop a resilient identity in Christ, and live out their unique vocation working together?

These three are most definitely intertwined. When people understand who they are through the lens of Baptism, then they can rely upon Christ. Then they are best suited to live out the callings God has given them because they understand that this is what God made them to be and to do.

We think it's helpful to think about these things in terms of the articles of the Apostles' Creed. Most Lutherans understand that Baptism is a Second Article gift by which we receive the saving work of Jesus and as a Third Article gift through which the Holy Spirit works. But it is also a First Article gift in that God restores us to live out the purpose for which we were created. When people understand not only from what they have been saved but also for what they have been saved, they are set free to serve their neighbors in the vocations God has given them because they know who they are without the vocations defining who they are.

What roles do pastors specifically have in helping the congregation to engage and teach well the final three practices?

Above all, the pastor has the responsibility to teach about these things to the entire congregation and to remind them consistently of these truths. In addition to this, the pastor can work with other leaders to ensure that these practices are being taught and confirmed through the overall ministry of the church. He can make sure that the Sunday School curriculum is supporting this, that the Sunday School teachers are prepared and equipped to

---

28 Large Catechism, Part V, paragraph 82, Concordia: The Lutheran Confessions, second edition (St. Louis: Concordia Publishing House, 2006).

reinforce it, and that the activities that the congregation is doing are also reinforcing this.

I also think that it is vital for the pastor to have a relationship with the youth in the congregation. They need to know him, and he needs to know them. He needs to spend time with them so that trust is gained and so that he understands their struggles and can speak to them appropriately. Teaching confirmation gives a great opportunity to really get to know young people, but then it's vital that he continue to interact with them regularly in their high school years and correspond with them during their college years as well.

How can the congregation work together toward healthy youth ministry?

Youth ministry should not be viewed as a separate thing from the ministry of the congregation but as a part of the whole.

I think there is a tendency to view ministries in separate boxes, and this tends to segregate people according to demographics. Now certainly there is a place for youth-specific events, but these should fit into the larger picture of what the congregation is about and seeking to do. When older members are connected with younger members, the older members become a source of encouragement, and they want the youth to be able to do things like attend the LCMS Youth Gathering.

When a church council is thinking about the big picture of ministry or even individual events, they should take youth into account and consider how they can be included and even encourage them to take on meaningful roles. In this way, the youth can grow up into positions of more responsibility and be mentored by older members. Then both young and old will be truly blessed.

Chapter 11

STRATEGIES FOR BIG IMPACT

You made it. Not to the end of the book, obviously, but through all seven practices. When Mark and Julianna present the seven practices in person, this is often where they see glassy, overwhelmed eyes from groups. This is understandable, and not just because of how fast we talk. There is a lot here to consider, including new ideas, strategies, and cultural shifts.

Let's start with a reminder of something we emphasized in the first chapter: healthy youth ministry isn't built on your effort. God loves the teens in our congregations and communities more than we can ever conceive. That God is at work in you, in parents, in supportive adults, in pastors, in commissioned workers, in staff, in lay leaders, and in more people. If we try to a build healthy youth ministry on our own, we will inevitably fail. When God is at work, we know that we will find success.

> LET'S START WITH A REMINDER OF SOMETHING WE EMPHASIZED IN THE FIRST CHAPTER: HEALTHY YOUTH MINISTRY ISN'T BUILT ON YOUR EFFORT. GOD LOVES THE TEENS IN OUR CONGREGATIONS AND COMMUNITIES MORE THAN WE CAN EVER CONCEIVE.

Isaiah 55:9–11 reads, "For as the heavens are higher than the earth, so are My ways higher than your ways and My thoughts than your thoughts. For as the rain and the snow come down from heaven and do not return there but water the earth, making it bring forth and sprout, giving seed to the sower and bread to the eater, so shall My word be that goes out from My mouth; it shall not return to Me empty, but it shall accomplish that which I purpose, and shall succeed in the thing for which I sent it."

God's Word doesn't return to Him empty. It accomplishes the things for which God sent it. The Holy Spirit works in and through Scripture to call, gather, and enlighten us. Remembering that youth ministry is God's work helps us put aside some of the pressure we put on ourselves or that we get from others. God doesn't need you to accomplish His good work. Jesus already did it all for us on the cross. Instead, God will use you in whatever you do to love and care for the teens and families in your congregation. What we do in ministry right now is God at work in us, and that is enough.

It can be easy to look at the seven practices as challenges for us to accomplish. Perhaps you are even tempted to gauge your success on how well you meet these practices. Instead, be reminded that youth ministry will always be imperfect. Yet God will continue to be faithful and fulfill His promises to you.

Some reading this book will have created a list of action items to bring to their youth ministry starting today. Others will have convinced themselves that healthy youth ministry is a lost cause. Still others are wavering on where to even start. As

God does His work in and through you, we want to direct that work in a way that has the greatest impact. Just as we would after our presentation, we would like to suggest some approaches that will multiply your effort to improve the health of your youth ministry.

We have witnessed that one of the most helpful ways to implement the seven practices involves identifying ways the practices readily interconnect with one another. This interconnection occurs where small, practical, and very strategic steps can have the biggest impact. In this chapter, we will identify these high-impact spaces in three ways. First, we will talk about identifying where practices overlap and create change that positively impacts multiple areas of ministry. Second, we will talk about how building relationships helps create change and a sense of working together to maximize efforts. Third, we will talk about how youth ministry works within the greater ministry of the congregation so that youth are cared for and valued across the life of the congregation.

These interconnected practices have a particular resonance that will amplify your adjustments and changes. We hope that in finding these places of interconnectedness, you can identify small, consistent actions where God works through your vocations and the vocations of others to make a big impact. In doing so, you can find strategies that help point young people to the Gospel now and in the future.

Every Practice Supports Other Practices

WHILE WE TALK ABOUT EACH OF THE SEVEN PRACTICES INDIVIDUALLY, THEY ARE ALL CONNECTED.

While we talk about each of the seven practices individually, they are all connected. Supportive adults bring warmth, challenge, and grace. Opportunities to serve help youth develop resiliency in their identity in Christ. Parents have a role in helping teens live out their unique vocation. In reading through these chapters, hopefully you have seen some themes repeated throughout. Every practice impacts the others, for good or for bad.

Understanding how the practices intersect with one another helps us make changes that benefit multiple practices at once. For example, a youth leader might want to increase the number of service opportunities for teens. She finds a local food pantry and takes youth there several times a year to clean, sort, and organize. This is a solid way to help give youth opportunities to serve and lead, and we celebrate that. But if we think about how the seven practices support one another, that youth leader might also decide to invite some adults in the congregation who are interested in getting to know the youth and put them into small groups as a way to help bridge awkwardness with a shared task. The youth leader might also include a Bible study and debriefing time to talk about how we welcome and share the Gospel with those who have financial needs while giving them dignity. Now our one event is helping engage in at least three practices rather than just one.

We see these overlapping ideas when we balance focusing specifically and deliberately on a single practice while at the same time looking at the larger overall picture. This back-and-forth will help you in a few important ways. First, it will make sure that you don't become hung up on improving one practice to the detriment of another. An example of this might be to focus so much on service opportunities for youth that you eliminate some of the time you should have spent helping them more deeply understand their baptismal faith. This almost always happens unintentionally and often without notice. Going back and forth between focusing on both the small and the larger pictures helps you maintain healthy practices while working to improve others.

Second, maintaining this balance helps you see where intersecting ideas in the practices lends to a strategy you would not normally expect. You may struggle to find ways for youth to understand their unique vocations and worry that they are compartmentalizing their faith. You can focus on teaching vocation and helping them practice being people of warmth, challenge, and grace. However, if you remember that one of the roles of engaged parents is to be supportive experts in their children, you may work through them toward the goal. Parents are with their children as they live out their vocations and can be equipped to teach them along the way. By engaging parents and their expertise in their child's interests and passions, you may find that together youth and their parents are more able to share the Gospel with their neighbors through word and deed.

Finally, looking at practices individually and then as a whole helps keep youth leaders from getting disheartened when changes don't work right away. Changes don't always come easily, and there is always some adjustment that needs to be made along the way. As the

AS THE HEALTH OF YOUR YOUTH MINISTRY INCREASES, CHANGES CAN TAKE LONGER THAN YOU HOPED, OR YOU MAY EVEN HAVE A SIGNIFICANT SETBACK. WHEN THAT HAPPENS, IT CAN BE HELPFUL TO LOOK AT WHERE YOU ARE FINDING SUCCESS IN YOUTH MINISTRY AND COME UP WITH WAYS TO USE WHAT IS WORKING TO BUILD IN AREAS OF GROWTH.

health of your youth ministry increases, changes can take longer than you hoped, or you may even have a significant setback. When that happens, it can be helpful to look at where you are finding success in youth ministry and come up with ways to use what is working to build in areas of growth. Because each practice is interconnected, when you move forward in one area, all the areas benefit, even when there are stumbles along the way.

If you want to be more focused on spots of interconnection between practices, it may be helpful to start by focusing on programs and opportunities you already have rather than creating something new. Consider where you see the seven practices reflected, or not, in these programs already. Celebrate your successes, but then consider where there might be low-hanging fruit. For example, we pray teens are already in worship to understand their baptismal faith and grow in Christ. Being supportive adults who champion teens who are disciples can overlap with that practice. Instead of starting something new, take advantage of the five or ten minutes before and after worship to increase connections between youth and supportive adults. Set a goal to greet each youth and his or her parents. This action builds relational connections and reinforces the idea that he or she is seen and can be a listening post for how the church can better serve youth and their families.

Any work to develop a healthy youth ministry will pay dividends. However, the efforts are amplified when multiple practices resonate with one another. As you read about each practice, certain ideas were repeated in multiple practices: relationships and environments that support a resilient identity in Christ, the need for strategic opportunities for service and leadership, and Christian education that engages students and doesn't shy away from difficult topics. The places where practices connect are especially potent because they improve the health of ministry in more than one way.

Relationships Fuel Healthy Youth Ministry

Throughout this book (and our book *Relationships Count*, which lays out our Millennials and the LCMS research in great detail), we have emphasized that healthy youth ministry that retains young people for life fosters relationships. You may be sick of hearing it, but it is important to say again here that the Gospel message is shared and lived out in the context of relationships. In order to be successful in any of the seven practices, you need to build healthy relationships. The more healthy, Christ-centered relationships you can build, the greater the impact you have on youth ministry.

Hearing the beautiful stories of LCMS congregational ministry in our research gave us a new appreciation for the role of relationships in the lives of God's people throughout Scripture. We know the divine relationship between Father, Son, and Holy Spirit and how God, in love, created and formed a relationship with His beloved creatures. We read how God used broken people and restores broken relationships between people and between Himself and sinners. We read how Jesus loved His disciples and how they interacted with one another. We love reading Paul's proclamation of the Gospel and doctrinal teaching in the book of Romans. However, Romans ends with a beautiful reminder of whom he had in mind as he wrote it. He spent the end of his letter to the Romans cherishing people by name, including Prisca and Aquila, who "risked their necks for my life" (Romans 16:4). (If only we knew more details!) God formed us for relationship!

The more healthy relationships in youth ministry, the better. Relationships can be formed through obvious connection but can also come from more unlikely places. When looking to add supportive Christian relationships in youth ministry, we can find them in the community, the congregation, church leadership, church staff, supportive adults, peers, and parents.

Building relationships with your community, particularly with service organizations and schools, can be difficult but rewarding. These relationships can help a youth ministry develop a consistent way to reach their community with the love of Jesus through long-term relationships that help expand the level of service youth can provide. Every community's school is going to fluctuate when it comes to openness to local youth ministries. For some, youth leaders are welcome to bring food or lead Bible studies. For others, those doors are tightly shut. It may take time, but developing a trusting relationship with local schools and other service organizations can open doors that allow you to care for youth who you might not otherwise be able to connect with.

Church members might not know a lot about the youth ministry program, yet broadly building relationships across the congregation can provide youth ministry with opportunities and resources that aren't available anywhere else. Youth ministry champions are often found in places where you would least expect them. Keeping the wider congregation up to date on what is happening in youth ministry might seem like a lot of work with little payoff. Yet keeping youth in the front of the congregation's mind helps make connections you might not otherwise be able to make. You may find older mentors who are passionate about the same things as youth. You may find that there are people connected to local businesses who can support youth. You may even find adults willing to pray consistently for youth even if they don't have time to be directly connected to the ministry.

CONGREGATIONAL LEADERSHIP CAN HELP CHAMPION YOUTH MINISTRY AND HELP YOUTH SEE HOW THEY ARE VALUED ACROSS THE CONGREGATION.

Congregational leadership can help champion youth ministry and help youth see how they are valued across the congregation. One way to build on these relationships is to come up with a shared vision or set of goals. These goals can include the seven practices or something similar. Study them together. As you do, be honest and open about how you are doing as a congregation. You are never going to get everyone to perfectly recite the seven practices, but you should be able to find some shared language and a shared direction. In building these goals, you can do more together and encourage one another as healthy changes are made.

Start by helping your pastor and other church staff build relationships with youth. Pastors may be trying to manage many responsibilities. It can be tempting to avoid adding more to what they are already expected to do. Youth leaders can play a big role in helping pastors understand what is going on in the lives of youth and what healthy youth ministry can look like. It can be helpful to give your pastor an understanding of the goals and language you are using. He will certainly have insight and direction that can help your leadership as well. More than that, invite pastors and other staff to youth ministry programming. Both they and the teens can benefit from spending time together, especially if the pastor isn't expected to be in charge. Seeing church staff in a relaxed setting can help youth feel more comfortable around them when needs arise. Involving your pastor in youth programming can build excitement around youth ministry and help him better connect God's Word with teens.

Seven Practices of Healthy Youth Ministry is not a program, which may be difficult for you to convey to other leaders. This book has a lot of content and nuance because enacting these practices will look different for every congregation. Don't rush through the seven practices. Take your time and take advantage of this book and other resources to help congregational leaders get a full understanding before you enact your goals. These shared visions and goals may change over the years based on staffing or the needs of youth. However, if you see positive outcomes for your ministry or the need to only make slight changes, you will know you have hit a sweet spot. If you are new to a youth ministry, reviewing the organization's visions and goals can help you familiarize yourself with the direction of your youth ministry.

Take the steps to regularly communicate with staff or boards if you haven't already. This communication builds trust and a shared knowledge of what is happening in youth ministry. It helps your ministry develop support and gives everyone a chance to celebrate success. Good communication across leadership increases the size of the network supporting youth and their families.

Supportive adults can focus on building relationships with youth, but there are additional benefits if they have relationships with one another. Adults who are connected to youth ministry can often develop a supportive community among themselves. We see this particularly when a group of adult leaders takes youth to a district or national event like the LCMS Youth Gathering. They talk together, find common ground—especially in caring for teens—and can be a sounding block when things are difficult. These adults can model what strong Christian friendships look like. Teens who have supportive adults build healthy youth ministry. If those supportive adults are also connected, it can be easier for them to serve long term and to be encouraged in their faith lives.

We haven't talked much about teen peer-to-peer relationships, but they are incredibly valuable to the health of your youth ministry. Adolescence is a time when friends become a high priority and begin to have a much stronger influence on actions and identity than ever before. When teens develop healthy relationships with one another, they build a supportive community of friends who can show both challenge and grace as they navigate their daily world. Christian friends can help youth navigate times when their faith is challenged or times when they have questions about their faith. Healthy youth ministry is much easier to work toward when youth genuinely like one another, can be honest with one another, and can welcome one another as they are.

Parents are a critical part of the team too. Parents have the primary role in modeling and teaching the faith. Your youth ministry's visions and goals are a great place to communicate and encourage parents in this responsibility. You can also let parents know how the congregation supports them or desires to support them in the future. This opens conversations about the church's care for them and their children as well as appropriate expectations for youth, and it invites parents to support the ministry. A healthy relationship between youth and parents and between parents and youth ministry can go a long way in multiplying ministry efforts.

In the Gospels, people were bringing children to Jesus, but they were hindered by the disciples. Jesus calls for children to come to Him and we should all seek to do just that. Congregational members, parents, supportive adults, peers, church workers, and more are brought together to support young people whose faith endures throughout their lifetimes. Not only should you not work toward enacting the seven practices alone but also you should remember that the more relationships you can build, the easier those seven practices will be to implement.

> IN THE GOSPELS, PEOPLE WERE BRINGING CHILDREN TO JESUS, BUT THEY WERE HINDERED BY THE DISCIPLES. JESUS CALLS FOR CHILDREN TO COME TO HIM, AND WE SHOULD ALL SEEK TO DO JUST THAT.

Healthy congregations (usually) have a healthy youth ministry.

While this book is focused on youth ministry, we know that youth ministry doesn't happen on its own. It is one part of a larger congregational ministry. A church with just middle school and high school students might be fun, but it wouldn't function for long (even with supportive adults). If we are thinking about healthy youth ministry, we have to consider the broader congregation.

When we hear stories about healthy youth ministry, it is nearly always in the context of a healthy congregation. It is difficult to maintain one without the other since they are so inextricably linked. If the congregation is struggling, you will see indicators in youth ministry as conflict, transition, and crisis carry over. It can be helpful to identify where you see environmental, historical, and other areas of impact from the greater congregation in youth ministry. If youth leaders want to approach those areas of conflict, it may mean first addressing some larger issues with leadership and staff. Likewise, if a congregation is flourishing, that momentum can spill over into youth ministry as well. A positive environment and encouraged volunteers can help increase energy and resources in youth ministry.

Rather than focusing exclusively on evaluating and incorporating the seven practices solely in youth ministry, consider implementing them with your congregation. Identify the congregation's strengths, history, and resources so you can help it foster relationships while studying God's Word and receiving Christ's gifts. You can conduct surveys or do interviews with the congregation as well as with the pastor, staff, newer members, and youth members. You may find that the seven practices (or other characteristics) are already in the culture of the congregation. You may also uncover places for growth that you could not previously see from your perspective.

It can be helpful to see where the seven practices are being used and practiced well in areas outside youth ministry. Perhaps you have a men's group that does a great job of showing warmth, challenge, and grace. Or maybe your children's ministry leadership has created some great strategies to engage parents. Consider how those strengths might connect with young people or how they might be carried into youth ministry. One of the easiest and best places from which to draw good ideas is the healthiest existing ministry in your own congregation.

Conversely, just because the focus of the seven practices is youth ministry doesn't mean that these practices cannot be incorporated in and bring health to other aspects of ministry as well. You may find ways to help build resiliency in a teen's identity in Christ. Don't keep that to yourself! There are most certainly older adults who might benefit from those teachings or activities. As you find or develop training and resources for youth leaders, parents, and supportive adults within youth ministry, be sure to make those available to adults widely outside of youth ministry. You may not know which adults outside of youth ministry might be interested or benefit. When resources are shared widely, it will only add people to the congregation who value teens, encourage parents, and champion youth ministry.

In chapter 8, we talked about coordinating Christian education across ages. Beyond just coordinating curriculum and helping in transitions, children's ministry will benefit from some, if not all, of the seven practices. Children also need supportive adults, engaged parents, opportunities to serve, and warmth, challenge, and grace. In fact, children's ministry may rely even more on supportive parents than youth ministry. This may be a group that you coordinate with more regularly as you consider how the seven practices can bring health to the congregation outside of youth ministry.

If you are struggling with your congregation's lack of support or interest in youth ministry, try connecting youth with service that is more up front in the congregation. Some congregations make teens the core of all their usher teams for worship. Though there are adults who help them, having teens interact with members and engage in service to the congregation publicly helps remind the congregation of the importance of supporting and caring for youth.

The Millennials and the LCMS study showed us that the broader congregation's handling of conflict, handling of mental health issues, and response to societal issues had an impact on how a young person felt about his or her congregation. When handled well and in a Christ-centered way, the congregation's response to these issues helped a young person value his or her congregational community and feel seen and cared for there. We found that young people felt the benefits of the caring congregational environment. As the Holy Spirit works to call, gather, and enlighten us around God's Word, how we speak and act toward one another, and particularly toward young people, can either draw them closer to or push them away from the Christian community.

FIGURE 8: IMPACT OF HOME CHURCH EXPERIENCES

Young adults who identify as LCMS Lutherans (and especially those who are active) have more favorable views of their home church.

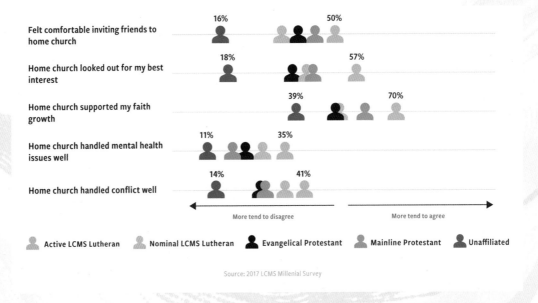

Source: 2017 LCMS Millenial Survey

How a church handled conflict and difficult issues did have an impact on the young person's perception of the church and consequently his or her connection to it. An environment of warmth, challenge, and grace is something you can develop in your youth ministry, but it will be far more effective if the whole congregation values these qualities as well. We want youth to feel comfortable bringing friends not just to fun youth ministry programming but to church events and even worship.

We are grateful for youth ministries that have taken and used the seven practices. In many of those cases, the seven practices did not stay in just the youth ministry. They permeated into other leadership and ministry areas and eventually the wider congregation. As they did, youth came to see that they are deeply valued not just in youth ministry but by the whole congregation.

Youth Ministry Is Messy

The word *practice* was chosen very specifically when we started to think of how we talk about youth ministry. We could have called these seven ideas, theories, actions, or qualities, but none of those indicated quite what we intended. These are goals we strive to enact rather than merits we achieve. They are the habits that guide our actions rather than idealized theories. The word *practice* means that there are skills that can be learned and mastered.

If you have worked with young people for a long time, you may have experienced them practicing a new sport or a new instrument. You have given encouraging praise while you watch fall after fall or listen to wrong notes in the wrong rhythm. We give praise and encouragement not just because we want young people to feel good. We do so because learning something new can be incredibly difficult, and it takes time to develop skills.

Practice is almost always messy. Practice is how we figure out why a particular play in a sporting event or a line of music continues to trip us up. Practice helps us break down and slow down enough to put together the smaller pieces of a skill. It might feel awkward or embarrassing. In the end, new skills come with greater ease, and we can advance to even more complicated skills as we gain competency.

Yet practice doesn't make perfect. It may be a saying, but reality shows us that perfection isn't realistic. Practice can help us improve. It can help us be more consistent and navigate changing circumstances. But just as we aren't going to be perfect basketball players or bassoon players, no matter how much we practice, there is no perfect youth ministry.

YOUTH MINISTRY IS ALWAYS CHANGING AS TEENS GROW, AS FAMILIES SHIFT, AND AS OUR CULTURE TRANSITIONS, SO WITH GOD'S HELP, WE CONTINUE TO PRACTICE.

We believe that every congregation can have a healthy youth ministry, but it will always take practice. Expertise will be gained, and it will become easier. Yet there will always be new skills to learn and people to engage. Youth ministry is always changing as teens grow, as families shift, and as our culture transitions, so with God's help, we continue to practice.

Maybe you can remember stepping into your first leadership role in youth ministry. You imagined highly attentive teens in small group discussions and meals full of pizza and laughter. There were games played cooperatively that built community and didn't cause injuries. Maybe you pictured youth who consistently walk a life worthy of the Gospel. Maybe you pictured high school seniors graduating and sharing thanks with a tearful congregation and older students mentoring freshmen.

We should call this "stock photo youth ministry" because it only exists in stock photos you purchase off the internet to populate your social media posts. It's an imagined reality staged to give you a false ideal of what healthy youth ministry should look like. The reality is that no youth ministry in this fallen world has ever looked like stock photo youth ministry.

Instead, youth ministry looks a lot more like the photos on your phone that you love but would never post on social media. Youth ministry includes teens who derail small group discussions in order to share a TikTok they saw and loved. Youth ministry is cleaning up after teens who ate all the pizza, left the veggie tray untouched, and drank two sips out of every soda before forgetting which one was theirs and getting another one. It involves games where teens vacillate between complete apathy and competing as though there is a million-dollar prize. Youth ministry is helping youth deal with a peer's suicide or the unexpected death of a loved one. Youth ministry is the heartbreak of watching youth make poor decisions and perhaps even walk away from the church.

Youth leaders tend to imagine and even plan for youth ministry that looks anywhere from enjoyable to as pristine as a stock photo. But that is not the reality of our broken world. When youth ministry gets gritty and real, that's not a failure on the part of leaders. It is simply a part of the vocation to which you are called by God, who wants you to love and care for teens as His dearly beloved children. All work toward healthy youth ministry is a challenge. Even maximizing your efforts and relationships will never make it quite what you imagine it could be.

WE DON'T DO YOUTH MINISTRY IN A PRISTINE BUBBLE. IT'S NOT A STOCK PHOTO. BUT PERHAPS IN THE BROKEN, FRUSTRATING, OR JUST PLAIN AWKWARD PARTS, WE GET TO SEE JESUS POWERFULLY AT WORK BRINGING LIFE AND SALVATION INTO OUR LIVES AND MINISTRY.

Youth ministry happens in the context of angsty teens whose attention spans are short, exhausted parents who are trying to do it all, and congregations that can sometimes be filled with all kinds of disagreements. We can't do this work without God. It is so important that we seek to care for young people in a way that doesn't lose sight of Jesus as the center of all we do. Our desire for the best working strategy can sometimes come at the cost of what is really important. Be willing to give up your perfectly conceived plan in order to keep your eyes focused on the redemption, forgiveness, and love that Jesus gives to His people. We don't do youth ministry in a pristine bubble. It's not a stock photo. But perhaps in the broken, frustrating, or just plain awkward parts, we get to see Jesus powerfully at work bringing life and salvation into our lives and ministry.

DISCUSSION QUESTIONS

1. As you read this book, where did you see practices overlap? Where can you get the most impact for your work in those areas?

2. What relationships might you be able to work on to help give a greater impact to your work on the seven practices?

3. How are you connecting with the pastor(s) and other staff at your church so that they are connected to youth ministry?

4. How is the strength of your overall congregation reflected in youth ministry? If it is not reflected, how might the strength be leveraged to support youth ministry?

5. How are you working with other ministry areas to cross-pollinate ideas around the seven practices?

Chapter 12

SO, NOW WHAT?

"So, now what?"

Our research team for the Millennials and the LCMS study had just finished two days of presentations on our findings. In a hotel ballroom, more than a hundred people gathered to hear about our three-part study, which took over a year to complete. We studied millennials who grew up in the LCMS and what motivated them to stay in the church or what caused them to leave the church. The work was intense. There were pockets of positive news, but there were also heartbreaking stories of young people who disconnected from the church.

The research provided us with far more raw data than we ever expected, and we were anxious to get responses from church leaders outside of our team. Analyzing our data up until just days before the presentation, we examined charts and pored over short answers. The PowerPoint presentation had more than two hundred slides.

We were exhausted. And in the dull hum of conversation during a break, someone approached Julianna to chat and asked, "So, now what?"

Julianna remembers staring, probably open-mouthed, for a bit too long. It was not the question she wanted to answer at that moment, but it was absolutely the correct question. Our team had been one part of a bigger approach to understand what was going on in our church body with demographics, evangelism, and retention. We learned so much thanks to the openness and honesty of the congregations and young people who participated. But we didn't have an action plan. We hadn't given congregations a way forward with the generations that follow the millennials.

In the months that followed, we continued to work with the data from the study in conversation with many youth ministry practitioners. The presentation was slowly whittled down to more like seventy slides as we found what information was most valuable and helpful to the church. In the end, Concordia Publishing House generously offered to partner with us to publish our findings in *Relationships Count*.

Even as our research continued to showcase our findings, the question "So, now what?" continued to linger. The research wasn't the end but rather a catalyst to clarify how we define healthy youth ministry. We wanted not simply to be able to say what not to do but to give language and definition of what we can strive to do for healthy youth ministry.

When that person asked, "So, now what?" years ago, Julianna has no idea how she answered. Frankly, she might not have answered. But she remembers feeling like the question made her brain reboot like an overwhelmed computer with too many programs running at once. It took time, but now she feels like she can answer that question with confidence. We know what healthy youth ministry can look like. Perhaps that will change, just as youth ministry always has, but there are next steps to suggest.

There are times in youth ministry when the only thing you as a youth leader can do is put one foot in front of the other. You are exhausted, overwhelmed, and doing your best to simply point young people to Jesus. In those moments, it may seem like far too much to ask for you to think big picture about the health of your youth ministry. If that is where you are at right now, God is working in and through you to care for the teens in your congregation and your community. You are doing enough.

There are also times when we need to ask ourselves, "So, now what?" The final chapter is going to focus on the actions you can take while answering that question. Before you put the book down, we want you to have a few next steps ready to go.

Ensure you have a resilient identity in Christ.

Serving in youth ministry can be exhausting at times, even when things are going well. Keeping up with communication, logistics, prepping Bible studies, and more can take over your time. At any moment, a teen could have a crisis that needs an additional level of attention. As youth leaders, we want to bring a clear and confident Gospel message into everything we do. In order to do that, we have to be well-rooted in our baptismal faith and our identity in Christ.

Colossians 2:6–7 says, "Therefore, as you received Christ Jesus the Lord, so walk in Him, rooted and built up in Him and established in the faith, just as you were taught, abounding in thanksgiving." Healthy youth ministry needs leaders, supportive adults, and parents who are rooted and built up in Christ to teach the next generation as they were taught. That means youth leaders need to regularly be in worship, prayer, Bible study, and confession and absolution.

Teens are incredibly perceptive and will often be the initial indicators that you might be lacking connection with Christian community and time spent learning about your faith. Julianna can recall times when comments made by youth helped her identify when her faith practice was faltering, even if they didn't know it. They would remind her that the group hadn't prayed during an event or a meeting. They complained or zoned out during a Bible study that was shallow and felt forced. All these comments were made in love, but they were also made with a level of brutal honesty only teens can have. In each of those cases, Julianna didn't blow off these comments but considered they might be indicative of a disconnect in her own spiritual practice. She took the comments as encouragements to prioritize her time in prayer and God's Word. It can be a positive sign when teens know they can and should be holding their youth leaders accountable as faithful Christians who are charged with their care.

There is a temptation to think of the church as a place where you serve and give of your gifts rather than a place where God serves you. While God certainly works through us in our vocations, if we want to care for others, we cannot lose sight of our own faith. If we do, it can be easy for our identities to shift away from being baptized children of God into youth leaders. This shift can lead to a lessening connection to the Gospel in youth ministry or burnout for the leader. We combat this shift by being connected to where God promises to be—in His Word and Sacraments.

If you are resilient in your identity in Christ, you will begin to sense when you are being stretched beyond your capacity. You may feel growing resentment rather than joy in your service. If you sense that you are starting to struggle or feel drained or overwhelmed, it is time to assess and make a new plan. As the adage says, "You cannot pour from an empty cup."

There are going to be phases when you may need to step back from youth ministry. This can be a difficult thing to admit when you love the teens in your congregation. You may feel they need you too much for you to take a season away. Your time with God cannot be set aside to keep up with the demands of youth ministry. Rather than pushing through, identify what your needs are and work with your team to give you the time and space you need. When you do need to step away, it is important to trust that God continues to work in and through other adults and parents to care for teens. Focus on your relationship with God, the greater congregation, and your family. Spend time being filled with God's Word and promises to you. In doing so, you will set an example for teens, showing them what it means to live out putting our saving faith first above all else.

Listen to young people early and often.

Data and information like the seven practices can give you valuable information, but this information doesn't usually come with instructions on how to use it. Think of it as a large map of a country. It's helpful for general knowledge and directions, but if you want to get to a specific house, you will need so much more.

Listening well to youth will give you the close-up information you need to apply what we have talked about here. Spend time asking the teens in your congregation and, as much as you can, the teens on the margins of your ministry and in your community questions.

The best strategies for youth ministry can fall apart if you don't listen to teens. For example, a youth leader might find that the number of attendees on Sunday evening is decreasing. He knows this is important information and wants to adjust the programming. He talks about it with his youth board. Someone concludes that the program must not be entertaining enough. With that conclusion, the board suggests that the youth leader should look for more elaborate games or a Bible study that includes more video clips. The numbers increase for a time, but then they return to where they were before. Frustrated, the youth leader puts more and more effort into finding ways to build in entertainment.

In the same example, if that leader would talk to his youth first, he might find an entirely different way forward. Perhaps it isn't at all about entertainment. Sunday evenings are when families are preparing for the week and when homework becomes a priority. Parents and youth would love to be involved in youth ministry, but they find the day and time difficult to prioritize. The solution may be to move youth events earlier in the day. After a time switch, numbers jump up and stay up. If we listen first, we may find that we are worried about things that aren't even on teens' radars. Or we may find that solutions we had not even considered are the best ones for the health of the ministry.

LISTENING TO YOUTH WHEN YOU ARE WORKING TOWARD HEALTHY YOUTH MINISTRY IS ONE WAY TO GIVE TEENS MEANINGFUL CONTRIBUTIONS.

Listening to youth when you are working toward healthy youth ministry is one way to give teens meaningful contributions. Youth have important insights and opinions that can direct your energy in productive ways. Listening to them also gives them ownership of what happens in the ministry. Teens have a unique perspective and contribute creative ideas that you can't get anywhere else. It requires asking questions and listening for genuine understanding and empathy. It means having to put aside your own conceptions and ego to truly understand their perspective.

Teens tend to be honest in their assessment of youth ministry, especially if trust and lines of communication have been open already. In listening to your youth, remember that you must be willing to take their insight, good or bad, even if you don't always agree with it. We aren't suggesting you should take every idea that pops into a teen's mind. Listening may mean hearing things you would rather not hear, such as skepticism, pain, or critique. In some cases, teens are going to be brutally honest about an idea or a program that you have spent lots of time and energy on. This criticism can quickly lead to hurt that can tempt you to become defensive or even combative. Rather than becoming defensive, let this give you an opportunity for honest dialogue, even when it is painful to hear.

Listening is not something you can do once and then be done with. It is something that you should do regularly, especially in times of change and growth. This is why it can be helpful to have teens on your leadership team in some way. It can be incredibly clarifying to put an issue or idea in front of youth and let them ask you questions or come up with potential solutions. Teens tend to forget that ministry has limitations, so actively listening to them can allow you to share why you do what you do.

Embrace the weird and glorious joy of youth ministry.

You could not pay us enough money to be teenagers today. Julianna struggled enough growing up as a nerd before it was cool, no less at a time when our computers had dial-up and our TVs didn't stream. Mark can't imagine how intense the embarrassment would have been if someone could record his high school dance moves and share them on social media. There is so much more for teens to worry about today and so many more opportunities to both succeed and fail. There are so many more aspects of identity to consider with pressure to both be yourself and fit in all at once. The places teens once counted on to support them are faltering.

You could not pay us any amount of money to convince us to become teenagers today, but you don't have to pay us anything to spend time and energy caring for the young people in our congregations. Perhaps you feel the same way. Many youth leaders volunteer for this ministry because they want to be the adults they know their younger selves needed in junior high and high school. We can empathize with how hard it is to be a teen, and we want to help navigate the treacherous time we call adolescence.

Some youth leaders are slightly embarrassed at how much they enjoy working with junior high and high school teens. It is not something everyone will understand. Teens are engaged one minute and over it the next. Their slang keeps you guessing, and their clothing choices can be questionable, like when they wear shorts in the dead of winter! They challenge authority and think they know everything.

But they also struggle with confidence and ask difficult, thoughtful questions about the world. Teens are multifaceted and weird, but for those of us whom God has equipped, serving them is an incredible joy. Loving youth ministry puts you in good company with thousands of others across the country who also want to care for, support, teach, and encourage teenagers.

LOVING YOUTH MINISTRY PUTS YOU IN GOOD COMPANY WITH THOUSANDS OF OTHERS ACROSS THE COUNTRY WHO ALSO WANT TO CARE FOR, SUPPORT, TEACH, AND ENCOURAGE TEENAGERS.

Teenagers aren't always easy to love. There will most certainly be someone in your youth ministry who you don't seem to connect with no matter how hard you try. Yet in the struggle, God provides unique opportunities for you to teach and guide teens in this vocation. Youth ministry will also give you opportunities to pause and think about your own life. You, too, will remember how you could be difficult to love as a teen. But parents and supportive adults didn't give up on you. You perhaps didn't have a family or a church that showed you warmth, challenge, or grace, but God kept you close to Him. Now, in your role in youth ministry, you can be a vessel through which God provides care, truth, and love that you didn't have. Regardless of your youth ministry experience, your investment in young people is an offering of thanksgiving to God for His faithfulness to you.

We conducted our research and started work on the seven practices before the COVID-19 pandemic. The value of relationships was obvious before, and we only saw it grow during the pandemic. Yes, relationships were often strained as the church struggled to engage Zoom, to maintain community while physically separated, and to navigate how to manage programs. However, the efforts of many faithful pastors, church workers, and lay leaders helped provide a cord that tethered people to hopeful, positive conversations and the Word of God. In many cases, church was a place that didn't allow a pandemic to sway people from their mission—to receive Christ's gifts, speak the love of Jesus, and display acts of mercy. We give thanks for church leaders across the country who were creative, caring, and resilient in showing young people the love of Christ through many ordeals.

We hope local congregations are attuned to the ongoing effects of the pandemic, technology, social media, and rampant individualism in the lives of young people. Even as our culture changes, God gives us opportunities to continue to engage youth for the sake of their salvation and health. As we talked about in previous chapters, loneliness and mental health struggles are hurting Gen Z, and that only grew during the pandemic. Youth (and adults) lost out on opportunities for meaningful face-to-face conversations, loving embraces, and social-emotional growth. We do not yet know all the impacts of the pandemic, but we can observe how social and emotional maturation slowed or was stunted by the lack of inputs and opportunities youth had during that time. Youth ministry can step into the space where technology and media leave teens lacking the experience of something real.

EVEN AS OUR CULTURE CHANGES, GOD GIVES US OPPORTUNITIES TO CONTINUE TO ENGAGE YOUTH FOR THE SAKE OF THEIR SALVATION AND HEALTH.

When we see our culture disconnect youth from one another and the world, we know that giving opportunities for true community centered in Christ can bring youth together. Those who care deeply for youth want to give them wide, loving spaces where they can grow and build connections that support them in joys and in difficulty. We can model and prepare teens to speak about a mental health crisis with friends and schoolmates. With the breakdown of so many key institutions that used to support youth, we hope that God will use local congregations and the LCMS to gather young people together and provide them with the hope and joy of Jesus.

Teens are not just weird sometimes; they will occasionally break your heart. After high school, they will more than likely move away. Perhaps you can catch them on your social media feed, but communication is harder as they grow up. Some are going to make choices that are contrary to God's Word. Your relationship with them in those moments, as difficult as it may be, may start to be one of their only tethers back to the Good News of Jesus. You may have youth return as adults who have started families of their own. In that moment, you will celebrate as you remember how quickly time passes. Teens are going to leave the church and not return. In that heartbreak, turn to God, who loves them and continues to look to bring them back to His fold.

Embracing your love of youth ministry has allowed you to take on a vocation of loving teens as you have been loved by Christ. We take them as they are, challenging them, pointing them to forgiveness in Christ, and encouraging them in their next steps. No matter how many youth you have in your congregation, you get to love them well and walk alongside them as they learn and grow. As you do, you will get opportunities to teach, to model, and to deeply impact their lives as the Holy Spirit works through you. It can be hard, but it also includes unmatched, glorious joy, so embrace your service with teens.

Focus and measure what matters.

Fostering healthy youth ministry takes focus, so it is important to clarify what we are focused on. If we focus on the programs rather than the people, we may end up spending time and energy on events that don't have a lasting goal. If we focus on ourselves rather than on teens, we can miss critical needs that the younger generation has. If we focus on a ministry that looks successful rather than one that prioritizes God and His Word, we can have a lot of flash with not a lot of retention.

One of the ways you can see what you are focused on is by how you are marking success. The most common marker of success is by looking at the number of teens you have in your congregation and regularly in your programming. Numbers are helpful. It may even seem like if we want everyone to know Jesus as Lord and Savior, numbers must be the goal. But healthy youth ministry can have fluctuating numbers for lots of reasons. Numbers don't tell the whole story.

Focusing on how to love young people in Jesus' name gives us a whole new set of markers for success. Different from numbers, these markers can help give us a better gauge of the overall health of our programs. You may want to look at the following markers:

- **Number of meaningful connections to congregational activities**

- **Willingness of teens to invite friends to church**

- **Parents' confidence level in talking about faith at home**

- **Teens' engagement in difficult conversations**

- **Retention in the church after confirmation and after high school graduation**

- **Congregational support for resourcing youth ministry with leaders, funding, physical space, and time**

While you will use these markers for success, you will need to articulate them well to leadership in the congregation so they, too, can understand the hoped-for outcomes. This prevents disappointment from missed expectations on either side of leadership. This is particularly true when leaders and supportive adults in the congregation are used to looking for numbers as their clearest marker of success. It is also important that you deliberately celebrate wins in a way that reminds youth, parents, supportive adults, and other youth ministry champions what you are trying to accomplish.

One of the things that can hamper your use of the seven practices is comparing your youth ministry to another youth ministry. Some youth leaders can focus too much on the ministries in nearby congregations. It is great to be open to new ideas or programs. However, comparing your ministry with other congregations only does you good if you are looking to feed your own ego or to feel disappointed in your own leadership. Keep your ears open for new and helpful insights, but keep your eyes forward on your own youth ministry rather than on others.

> COMPARING YOUR CURRENT YOUTH MINISTRY TO A PAST YOUTH MINISTRY POINTS YOUR YOUTH MINISTRY IN THE WRONG DIRECTION. WE CANNOT RECAPTURE THE PAST. WE CAN ONLY LEARN WHAT TO TAKE FORWARD INTO THE FUTURE.

You may find yourself or other leaders wishing for a time long ago when youth ministry seemed easier. It is easy to think of the past as a time when parents were more involved, teens were more respectful and receptive, and the church had more resources. In some ways, this is true. In other ways, it is a fantasy. Comparing your current youth ministry to a past youth ministry points your youth ministry in the wrong direction. We cannot recapture the past. We can only learn what to take forward into the future.

Focusing on loving young people in Jesus' name means that you are flexible to meet youth and families where they are. If the Gospel is the priority, then specific programs can come and go, even if you enjoyed them for a time. You can even let go of things that were successful with a different generation or with different resources. Programs serve to share God's Word and keep teens connected to God's church rather than the other way around. Flexibility means we resource programs that work and move on to something new when programs no longer meet our goals.

If Jesus is the focus, we know that our faith impacts every part of our lives. We can ensure that what we do in youth ministry guides youth to see how their faith should be their top priority. We can consider how this looks in their lives and walk beside them. While we do not change God's Word to fit our circumstances, we can help youth see how it is relevant all the time.

If you stay focused on the most important thing, other things will fall into place. Flashy, self-serving, or long-past-its-expiration-date youth ministry often means you have lost the focus. God works in those spaces, but you may find yourself struggling with disappointment. Strive for a healthy, Christ-centered youth ministry that is focused on God and His promises for us so that young people can become life-long disciples.

Move forward.

With so much information, deciding what to do next can feel like a struggle. In a situation where there are many options, your brain can go into choice overload. You might assume that having seven different practices to focus on and a number of different approaches would be a good thing. However, there is a documented difficulty when you are given too many choices.[29] Even the list of potential places to start in this chapter can feel like too much. We may spend too much time considering potential choices, which can cause us to get stuck.

Fighting choice overload means taking steps to get started. Take some time to listen first to youth and assess your current ministry. Once you have, choose what to do first. Once you do, don't change your mind or start over again until you feel confident you have completed the tasks as well as you can.

If you get distracted by the other things you could be doing, you will likely end up either spreading yourself too thin or jumping back to square one over and over without letting your plans fully develop and take root. If you are listening to youth and focusing on the right things, don't be distracted by other things or even other ministries. Stay the course until you start to feel confident in your practice enough to try something else.

Approach your practice in youth ministry like you would learning a new instrument. If you are learning an instrument, you have lots of music options to choose from as you practice. But if you practice a different piece every time, your improvement will be stunted and you won't have a single piece that you can play well. Instead, focusing on one piece of music at a time helps you get to a place of competency.

Ministry books can be incredibly helpful, but they have some downfalls. One of those is that all the ideas and concepts in the book stay there unless you decide to put them into action. So before you close this book and put it on the shelf, we want you to have some kind of next step. Who are you going to share this book with? Who do you need to talk to next? What small changes can you start to implement

---

29 "Why Do We Have a Harder Time Choosing When We Have More Options?" The Decision Lab (website), https://thedecisionlab.com/biases/choice-overload-bias (accessed March 13, 2023).

that might get the ball rolling? As we have said before, smaller, consistent changes can have an impact, but reading this book alone may not bring about any discernible change other than filling up a bookshelf.

You can begin at many points. The important part is starting. Movement begets movement. As you begin, we pray that God will build a team and momentum that increases your care for the young people in your congregation and your community.

> WE PRAY THAT GOD WILL BUILD A TEAM AND MOMENTUM THAT INCREASES YOUR CARE FOR THE YOUNG PEOPLE IN YOUR CONGREGATION AND YOUR COMMUNITY.

Champion long-term change.

Change isn't easy, but it is inevitable. When writing this book, we looked at a lot of the history of youth ministry in the LCMS. We found a story of change after change. While God's Word stays the same, how the Gospel is proclaimed and how young people are cared for in the church will change. There are ways to successfully shift ministry without losing sight of what's important or of valuable practices and traditions. We can change without moving away from our God, the solid rock who never changes.

Implementing the seven practices will mean bringing change to your youth ministry and your congregation. As you champion these changes, make sure you are communicating clearly and frequently with everyone who has a stake in youth ministry. You need to paint a picture that explains where you are headed and why. Be willing to answer questions and be flexible enough to get even the most doubtful on board. The more you can do this, the easier each subsequent change will be.

It is possible that as you have been reading this book, you have felt affirmed that your youth ministry is doing an excellent job caring for the young people in your congregation and your community. You may know from listening to your teens that you are focused on the right goals and have developed practices and programs for healthy youth ministry. If you have, LCMS Youth Ministry would love to hear what that looks like for you. (And that is a serious ask!) We know some ministries have been following these practices for decades, and we are grateful for how God is working through them.

Even if you feel your youth ministry is engaging in all seven practices right now, that doesn't mean it will always stay that way. Every year, youth ministries welcome new teens and graciously send older teens into adulthood. Often, your leadership will change, either through new board elections or even through staff changes. Small changes and adjustments will always be necessary, or entropy will set in. Even the healthiest ministry needs to be fully engaged in assessment and adjustment over time.

If you read something in this book or hear something from your teens that makes you think that perhaps you have some work to do toward healthy youth ministry, you are not alone. In fact, we would wager a guess that you are in the majority. If that's the case, it is time to consider what changes you want to make. Be careful not to make changes just for the sake of changing. Intentionality is key as you work to shift programming and implement new ideas.

Some changes will be small or short-term. These small adjustments will allow you to test out a variety of programming pieces to help you find what resonates most with youth. These should not be quick fixes that cover up bigger issues but small adjustments that provide good information for greater future change. For example, it is good to switch up small groups to see what dynamics between ages and genders work best for your current group. Sometimes it is helpful to adjust the typical schedule of a youth night to see if these types of adjustments bring better engagement. Experimenting can often give you interesting and valuable results.

Be prepared to put your time and energy around bigger changes that will have a long-term impact. There can be pain in these changes, but when they are done with clarity and purpose, they can free up ministry for something better. This can happen when you let go of a legacy program that no longer serves teens well or when you change how your leadership team functions. There will always be pushback, but change done well means there is something more on the horizon. Consider not just the teens you have now but the younger kids currently in your Sunday School classrooms. They will be in youth ministry soon enough. Consider your teens as they begin their careers and families. Changes big and small that are made for the long term help us continue to point to Jesus in all we do.

CONSIDER THE ADULTS WHO IN BIG AND SMALL WAYS IMPACTED YOUR LIFE AND WHO SHARED THE LOVE OF JESUS WITH YOU. WE KNOW THAT GOD GIVES GROWTH, EVEN WHEN WE ONLY GET TO BE ONE PART OF THE PLANTING.

You might never see the results of your work in youth ministry. Youth leaders get a short time with teens, and often teens can't see the impact of a leader's work in the moment. A youth leader's time might be short, but that doesn't mean it can't be powerful. Consider the adults who in big and small ways impacted your life and who shared the love of Jesus with you. We know that God gives growth, even when we only get to be one part of the planting.

There is always more to do and learn.

When we first developed the seven practices, we asked many people to give us feedback and input. We changed, tweaked, added, and took things off. We debated order and language to make sure that we said exactly what we intended. At one point, our staff took over a hotel breakfast room late at night to splice out our wording for the first seven practices magazine. (That was the eventual basis for this book.) We were spurred on to dig even deeper into Scripture and theology to learn more about God's desire for young people. Our first few presentations were nerve-racking as we tried to solidify concepts and communicate them well.

After a year of talking about the seven practices, we sat down to reassess what we had learned. With every presentation we gave, there were thoughtful questions that helped us clarify our language. We worked with experienced leaders to see how they saw the seven practices and how they reflected their ministry settings. If you were a part of one of those first presentations, you might notice that we have changed and moved pieces since we first began to share. We, just like you, are always learning and growing in how we steward the young people placed in our care.

If you call our office today and inquire about healthy youth ministry, we will answer with confidence. We will point you to these seven practices and the many youth leaders who are successfully using them in their ministry. Perhaps now you will be able to answer that question as well. We are grateful for every person, study, piece of theology, and passage of Scripture that have shaped these practices so far. We look forward to the feedback from this book to inform and shape how we talk about youth ministry.

THERE ARE CHALLENGES BEFORE US EVERY DAY, BUT WE KNOW THAT GOD, WHO MADE US AND SAVES US, IS CONSTANT. HE ALWAYS MAKES GOOD ON HIS PROMISES NO MATTER WHAT COMES OUR WAY, AND WE CAN BE SECURE IN OUR GIFT OF FAITH IN JESUS.

The reality is that we may still shift and change the seven practices, though it may be much harder now since we have a book. We can look back to Walther League or to the early days of Lutheran Youth Fellowship and know much is the same and much has changed. These practices are never set in stone because how we care for young people is always changing. There is so much we don't know about the long-term effects of technology, social media, COVID-19, and other cultural events that affect teens. The next generation is coming into junior high soon, and there is so much we don't know about how they will impact our world and our church.

There are challenges before us every day, but we know that God, who made us and saves us, is constant. He always makes good on His promises no matter what comes our way, and we can be secure in our gift of faith in Jesus. Just as we want our youth to be lifelong learners of the faith, LCMS Youth Ministry is committed to constantly learning from you and from God's Word how to guide, care for, and engage young people.

Our desire is not to come across as experts who give you the only right way to do youth ministry. We want all congregations to value youth ministry and to earnestly seek how to love their youth well in Jesus' name. We celebrate your success and lament when sin, death, and the devil strike. In all of this, we learn together. Let this book cheer you on, give you wisdom, and spring you forward into new ideas. Let us challenge one another to see how God can work through our vocations.

We will continue to keep you in our prayers as you care for the young people of your congregation. God is faithful, and He will guide us together until the end.

DISCUSSION QUESTIONS

1. How are you and the other youth leaders on your team ensuring youth have a resilient identity in Christ?

2. What is one small step you can take in your youth ministry before you put this book on your shelf?

3. How are you preparing and planning for changes big and small that might bring additional health to your youth ministry?

4. How well are you listening to the youth in your congregation? How well are you listening to the youth "on the fringe" of your congregation? What tool or process might you implement to listen better or more often to their voices, concerns, and needs?

5. What markers, other than head count numbers, can help you gauge the health of your youth ministry? Who else (pastor, staff, boards, parents) should be invested in that conversation or assessment?

Appendix 1

AT-HOME DISCUSSION GUIDE FOR THE 40 END GOALS FOR YOUTH MINISTRY

Introduction

The 40 End Goals are statements we pray teens will know and personalize by the time they graduate high school. They aren't the whole of Scripture or Lutheran theology, but they are critical pieces of understanding our baptismal faith. We pray young people hear these key tenets in worship, Bible study, youth ministry, and, most especially, in their homes. Homes can be powering places to teach and apply these biblical truths in young people.

Below is a guide to help you discuss the 40 End Goals with your teen. Here are a few things to keep in mind:

You aren't doing this alone. Be sure to center discussions in Scripture. Use *The Lutheran Study Bible* (or another Bible), the Small Catechism, and trusted digital resources like www.youthesource.com and lcms.org. Reach out to your pastor, church workers, and other supportive adults as needed.

These are meant to be back-and-forth conversations. Don't dominate or teach at teens. Instead, listen well and ask good follow-up questions.

There is a good chance that your teen will have difficult questions or respond differently than you might expect. Treat those moments with warmth, challenge, and grace. Keep the conversation going rather than shutting it down.

Be willing to be vulnerable. As it's appropriate, share your questions and tell your personal stories of failure, grace, and joy.

There is no "right way" to have faith conversations in your home. We know that young people who are active in the LCMS today reported higher levels of being able to have difficult conversations about life and faith in their homes than those who left the church. Just trying to have these kinds of conversations can be a step forward in helping a young person better understand their baptismal faith and develop resiliency in their identity in Christ.

DISCUSSION GUIDE

Have everyone share a high (celebration), a low (disappointment), and something surprising that happened today.

Read one of the 40 End Goals of youth ministry (found at the end of chapter 8 of this book).

Discuss the following questions:

1. What does this tell us about God? about ourselves? about our Christian community? about our world?

2. When have you understood this differently or more clearly?

3. How have you struggled or how do you struggle with this?

4. Where else in God's Word do we hear something similar? Does this remind you of any Bible accounts? of any part of the Small Catechism?

5. How does this remind us of our sin? How does this remind us of the Good News of Jesus?

6. How can God's truth impact how we make choices and live day to day?

Discuss prayer requests you and your youth might have for that day. Pray together.

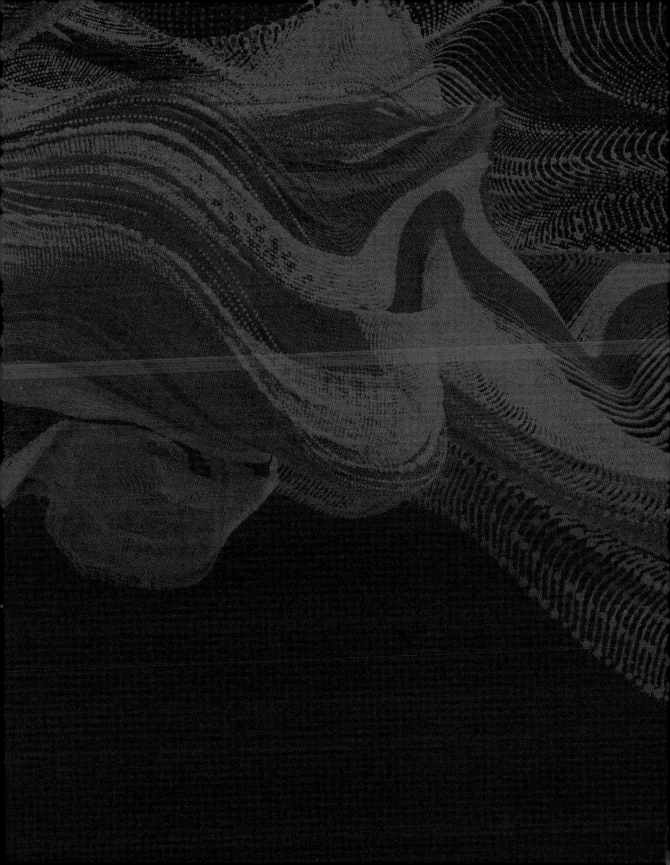

SEVEN PRACTICES WITH SUBPOINTS

Seven Practices of Healthy Youth Ministry

Congregations have . . .

Warmth, Challenge, and Grace

Congregations foster an open and honest environment where youth share joys, questions, crises, and doubts, knowing God's Word will be spoken in love.

Congregations share personal stories of grace, failure, challenge, and joy.

Congregations are willing to engage in tough spiritual conversations.

Congregations have a dedicated, developmentally appropriate space for youth where they grow as disciples with their peers.

Supportive Adults

Supportive congregations seek to connect every youth with at least five engaged Christian adults.

Supportive adults deliberately invest and value long-term, intergenerational relationships.

Supportive adults prepare for and respond to celebrations, transitions, and crises.

Supportive congregations have adults who champion young people and dedicate time and energy to developing teens as disciples of Jesus Christ for life.

Engaged Parents

Engaged parents prioritize faith development by encouraging daily faith practices, especially during times of transition.

Engaged parents invest in the lives of their children by understanding their child's vocation and the culture around them.

Engaged parents participate in worship, personal spiritual practices, and service.

Supportive congregations provide parents encouragement and support from other Christian adults.

Opportunities to Serve and Lead

Congregations identify gifts and skills in youth that can be used in service, leadership, and vocation inside and outside the church.

Congregations invest in youth by providing consistent opportunities for meaningful contributions.

Congregations engage and support youth in service inside the congregation, in the community, and beyond.

Congregations empower young people to be load-bearing leaders by providing training, mentors, and space to learn.

Congregations help all young people . . .

Deeply Understand Their Baptismal Faith

Youth live as forgiven sinners with the promise of eternal life through Jesus' death and resurrection.

Youth recognize the work of the Holy Spirit, who brought them to faith, gathers them into God's family, and works through them.

Youth regularly worship, study the living and active Word of God, pray together, and receive the Lord's Supper.

Youth are provided with deliberate age-specific opportunities to move toward key outcomes for young Lutheran Christians. (Examples are outlined in the 40 End Goals.)

Develop a Resilient Identity in Christ

Resilient youth identify with the life and mission of the Christian Church and seek to serve others.

Resilient youth remain humbly confident in their faith in the face of crisis and transition.

Resilient youth can build relationships with those different from themselves and navigate disagreements in a humble, loving way.

Resilient youth are lifelong learners who face doubt and challenge by turning to God's Word.

Live Out Their Unique Vocation

Youth understand their roles as Christ's hands and feet in their church, home, community, and other areas of vocation.

Youth reach out to their neighbors in word and deed to love and share the Good News of Jesus.

Youth serve and lead in their congregation and community.

Youth seek to be warm, challenging, and grace-filled to their community and peers.

Youth are encouraged to pursue church work vocations as it fits their gifts and skills.